Alvin, Virginia, Robert Silverstein
Hepatitis
(Diseases & People)

616.3

DATE	ISSUED TO

HEPATITIS

—Diseases and People—

HEPATITIS

Alvin, Virginia, and Robert
Silverstein

ENSLOW PUBLISHERS, INC.

44 Fadem Road   P.O. Box 38
Box 699   Aldershot
Springfield, N.J. 07081   Hants GU12 6BP
U.S.A.   U.K.

Library of Congress Cataloging-in-Publication Data:

Silverstein, Alvin.
 Hepatitis / Alvin, Virginia, and Robert Silverstein.
  p. cm. — (Diseases and people)
 Includes bibliographical references and index.
 ISBN 0-89490-467-1
  1. Hepatitis—Juvenile literature. [1. Hepatitis. 2. Diseases.]
 I. Silverstein, Virginia B. II. Silverstein, Robert A. III. Title. IV. Series.
 RC848.H42S49   1994
 616.3'623—dc20   93-48734
                                                          CIP
                                                           AC

Printed in the United States of America

10 9 8 7 6 5

Illustration Credits: ©1992 Amethyst/Custom Medical Stock Photo, pp. 57, 97;
©1993 Amethyst/Custom Medical Stock Photo, p. 94; AP/Wide World Photos, p.
8; ©1992 B.S.I.P./Custom Medical Stock Photo, p. 54; Centers for Disease
Control, p. 34; CNRI/Science Photo Library, Custom Medical Stock Photo, pp.
33, 86; ©1990 Custom Medical Stock Photo, p. 31; Drug Enforcement
Administration, p. 46; ©1989 Fotex/Custom Medical Stock Photo, p. 81; Fox
Chase Cancer Center, pp. 23, 102; ©1988 Kelvin Beebe/Custom Medical Stock
Photo, p. 63; Merck & Co., Inc., p. 77; National Archives, p. 15; New Jersey
Newsphotos, p. 83; Reuters/Bettmann, p. 44; Science Photo Library/Custom
Medical Stock Photo, p. 65.

Cover Illustration: Zuber/Custom Medical Stock Photo.

Contents

Acknowledgments

The authors would like to thank Dr. Hari Conjeevaram of the Liver Disease Section of the National Institutes of Health for his careful reading of the manuscript, his generous help, and his encouragement.

Thanks also to Dr. Rafael Harpaz of the Centers for Disease Control for his kind help and valuable insights, as well as to all those who supplied photographs and information for the book.

HEPATITIS

What is it? An inflammation of the liver caused by hepatitis A, B, C, D, or E viruses; drugs; or other factors.

Who gets it? People of all ages, both sexes, all around the world.

How do you get it? Hepatitis A and E are spread by water or food contaminated by feces. Hepatitis B, C, and D are transmitted similarly to AIDS: by blood (transfusions or sharing needles with an infected person), by sexual activity (especially hepatitis B), and by infected mothers passing it to their children.

What are the symptoms? Jaundice (yellowing of the eyes and skin), loss of appetite, nausea and vomiting, fever, extreme fatigue, stomach pain, and joint pain.

How is it treated? Mainly by rest and treatment of symptoms. Interferon (an immune booster) is used to treat hepatitis B and C. Antiviral drugs are used experimentally. When liver damage is severe and life-threatening, a liver transplant may be performed.

How can it be prevented? Vaccines are available for hepatitis B, and health authorities recommend vaccination of all children. Good sanitation practices can help prevent hepatitis A and E. Screening of donor blood is helping to prevent transmission of hepatitis B and C through transfusions. Avoiding high-risk behaviors such as needle-sharing and sex with multiple partners can help prevent hepatitis B and C.

Wynonna and Naomi Judd, country music's dynamic duo, performing in concert together.

1

The Disease
That Turns You Yellow

n December 1991 the Judds—country music's dynamic
mother-daughter duo—gave a joint concert that was their
last for more than two years. Naomi Judd and her
daughter Wynonna had become immensely popular with
country music fans, collecting six gold records and four
Grammys. But at the peak of their fame, Naomi announced
that she would no longer be able to perform. She needed to
use all the energy she had to cope with a life-threatening
illness: hepatitis. Naomi Judd described her chronic condition
as "kind of like having a monster in your basement."[1]

Strictly speaking, hepatitis is not really a disease; it is an
inflammation of the liver that can be caused by various things,
including a number of viruses—called hepatitis A, B, C, D,
and E. It is best known for causing the skin and the whites of

the eyes to turn yellow. Hepatitis may be very mild or it can be quite severe. Most people recover on their own, but some never recover and can continue to suffer—as well as spread the illness to others—for the rest of their lives. Others don't even know that they have hepatitis but they are nevertheless contagious.

Hepatitis can also kill. Few people die from it right away, but years later some develop serious liver problems, such as cirrhosis and liver cancer. Hepatitis is the leading cause of liver cancer in the world, and the second greatest cause of cancer overall. (Smoking is first.) Worldwide, hepatitis is a leading cause of death. Hepatitis B, one of the most common forms, kills 1.2 million people each year, tying it with malaria as the eighth biggest killer.[2]

The problem is growing in the United States, too. Only about 70,000 cases of hepatitis are reported each year, but the real numbers are much higher. Nearly half a million Americans are thought to be infected with hepatitis yearly, and the amount of illness and death caused by it is approaching that of AIDS in America.[3]

Traditionally, hepatitis has not received very much attention. One reason is that it is not usually as dramatic an illness as, say, AIDS, polio, or smallpox. Most people recover completely on their own, and those who do suffer serious consequences usually don't develop them until years later. "These viruses generally don't kill you quickly," says Dr. Jay Hoofnagle, a hepatitis expert at the National Institutes of Health. "These are infections that people acquire when they're young, some through sexual activity [and IV drug abuse], and that kill them in their fifties."[4]

In addition, most people don't think they are at risk for developing hepatitis. In the past it was thought of—even by most doctors and scientists—as a disease of the poor (due to unhealthy sanitation conditions) or was linked to intravenous drug users or sexually active male homosexuals; or it was regarded as a risk factor for people who received blood transfusions. But the truth is that "hepatitis B is more common than AIDS and far more contagious," says Dr. David A. Shafritz, director of the Liver Research Center at the Albert Einstein College of Medicine in New York City.[5] Now hepatitis is spreading more widely into the general population. In fact, scientists don't even know how 30 to 40 percent of the people with hepatitis B and C became infected.

Scientists did develop a vaccine against hepatitis B more than a decade ago. But the number of hepatitis cases in America has not decreased. In fact, the number has gone up dramatically.

While the annual hepatitis statistics are growing, so is our knowledge about this family of diseases. Scientists have developed more accurate diagnostic tests. Other tests have helped to greatly reduce the spread of hepatitis through blood transfusions. Although there are not many effective ways to treat hepatitis, there are vaccines available to prevent many cases from developing in the first place. The problem is, however, that most people do not know enough about hepatitis or the behaviors and lifestyles that increase the risk of developing it; and too few of those at risk are receiving the vaccine.

Doctors are hopeful that new medical breakthroughs, combined with better public education about hepatitis, will help to control—and someday eliminate—this important health problem.

2

Hepatitis Through the Ages

octors have known about hepatitis, a condition that causes the skin to turn yellow, since ancient times. Over the past twenty-two centuries, epidemics were occasionally noted in civilians, but hepatitis most often occurred under wartime conditions. Napoleon's armies were hit with an outbreak; both armies of the American Civil War were struck hard; and hepatitis helped change the course of several battles during World War I. But no one knew what caused hepatitis, and it wasn't until World War II that doctors found out it could be transmitted from one person to another through blood.

During World War II there were 200,000 documented cases of hepatitis among U.S. soldiers; 352 died. Five million Germans are said to have contracted the disease, as well.[1] The epidemic caught everyone by surprise, but health officials quickly figured out what must have caused the illness in the United States soldiers.

In 1942 seven million doses of a new yellow fever vaccine were sent to the U.S. Army. Health officials were trying to prevent an epidemic of this disease, which sometimes strikes under war conditions. The vaccine prevented the yellow fever, but many soldiers came down with "yellow jaundice" (a name often used for hepatitis because of the yellowish tint it gives the skin).

It turns out that the vaccine had been prepared using blood serum contaminated with a virus that causes hepatitis. But no one knew that at the time because there were no tests available to detect the virus. This epidemic changed the way hepatitis was perceived by the world. After World War II, hepatitis was no longer thought of as just a disease of overcrowded and unsanitary conditions. If it could be transmitted in a vaccine, then anyone could get it, through blood transfusions or other exposure to blood.

The First Pieces of the Puzzle

In the mid-1950s Saul Krugman, a professor at New York University Medical School, was contacted by the Willowbrook State School for retarded children in Staten Island. Hepatitis was epidemic at the institute, and the hospital officials wondered if Dr. Krugman could help. In just a few years, the NYU researcher helped end the Willowbrook epidemic. At the same time he discovered many things about hepatitis,

During World War II, an epidemic of hepatitis is said to have struck 5 million German and 200,000 American soldiers. This epidemic greatly changed the perception of hepatitis worldwide.

which eventually led to a vaccine that has prevented millions from getting the disease. However, his efforts also resulted in a bitter controversy.

Because no one knew what caused hepatitis, Dr. Krugman was faced with a difficult task in trying to eliminate it. Most scientists thought it was caused by a virus. Even today there are not many effective treatments for viral diseases, and in the 1950s there were *no* antiviral drugs available. Prevention is the key to controlling viral diseases. Usually that means using a vaccine. But in order to produce a vaccine, one has to find the virus that the vaccine is supposed to work against.

Dr. Krugman's experiments began in 1956 and lasted for seven years. "It was inevitable that all newly admitted children would come down with hepatitis; they couldn't escape it. So we realized that the only way we could learn something about the disease which would eventually lead to prevention was by studying small groups of children and actually exposing them to the same Willowbrook strain of hepatitis that they were going to live with anyway as soon as they came into the institution," Saul Krugman later explained, after news of his experiments sparked a hotly debated controversy.[2]

When the body is exposed to viruses, it builds special proteins called antibodies, which are custom-designed to attack that particular type of virus. The next time the body encounters that kind of virus, the antibodies spring into action, preventing the person from becoming infected again. (In medical terms he or she is immune to that viral disease.) Dr. Krugman showed that injecting antibodies that other people had built up against hepatitis gave temporary protection to those who had not yet been exposed to the virus.

Dr. Krugman also showed that once a person got hepatitis, he or she was immune. But then something surprising happened. Some of the children who had gotten the disease suffered a second attack within a year. The NYU researcher wondered whether the second attack could be due to a different virus. Hepatitis had traditionally been associated with overcrowded, unsanitary conditions. But the soldiers in World War II had gotten the disease from contaminated vaccines. Could there be two different diseases with similar symptoms?

In 1964 Dr. Krugman began another set of experiments that lasted three more years. He fed eleven children a mixture containing blood drawn from a large number of hepatitis victims at Willowbrook. After thirty to sixty days, ten of the eleven had come down with hepatitis. Dr. Krugman drew a blood sample from one of the infected boys and labeled it MS-I.

Six months later the same children were *injected* with the virus mixture. Within two months some of the children became infected again. The second infection took longer to show up, and it took longer to get over than the first oral infection. Dr. Krugman took another sample of blood from the same boy and labeled it MS-2. Now he had two blood samples, MS-I and MS-2, which he believed contained two different viruses that caused hepatitis. The first had been transmitted by mouth (orally) and the second by contaminated blood.

In the third trial, which involved fourteen children, eight children were injected with MS-I, the oral hepatitis infection. Seven of the eight children became infected within a month. All of the other six children became infected, too, even though they had not received any injections. They had caught the virus just from contact with the other seven.

Then fourteen more children were selected; nine were injected with the MS-2 hepatitis infection. In a month and a half seven of the nine became infected, but only two of the five children who hadn't been injected developed hepatitis. The researchers on the NYU team concluded that there were two different viruses, one that was highly contagious by contact, and another that was highly contagious through blood but less contagious by contact. Dr. Krugman hadn't identified the hepatitis viruses, but he did show that they caused two separate diseases. Eventually the MS-I and MS-2 viruses became known as hepatitis A virus (HAV) and hepatitis B virus (HBV), respectively.

Discovering a Way to Detect Hepatitis

The next piece of the hepatitis puzzle, like many scientific achievements, was discovered partly by chance. Disease researcher Dr. Baruch Blumberg didn't have hepatitis in mind at all when he started his monumental hepatitis research. He was trying to find out why people of different races react differently to disease organisms. Just as humans can have

A QUESTION OF ETHICS

When Dr. Krugman published his results, they caused quite a stir. In 1967 a New York state senator attacked the researcher for his "unethical, immoral and illegal" experiments that violated "the legal and moral rights of the children, who are being used as guinea pigs."[3] He introduced a bill to ban research using children.

Dr. Krugman pointed out that the children would have gotten hepatitis at the institution anyway, and that his team had virtually eliminated the disease there. If there had been such a law in the 1950s, children would still be dying of measles and crippled by polio. The vaccines that brought these diseases under control had to be tested on children—they were the ones being struck by these diseases. Moreover, only children whose parents consented to their child's involvement were included in the hepatitis studies. The children involved in the research lived in special wards that were much better than the overcrowded ones in which the other children lived.

The medical community defended and praised Dr. Krugman for his efforts, and the New York State Senate bill was defeated. But ethical controversies of this kind still rage today in connection with diseases such as AIDS.

different blood types, he believed that there must be slight differences in our genes that control our immune systems, causing people to react differently to diseases.

Dr. Blumberg began collecting blood samples from hundreds of thousands of people around the world. To find genetic differences, he looked for proteins that were found in some blood samples, but not others. Genes create proteins, so differences in blood proteins are a reflection of genetic differences. Dr. Blumberg decided to test the blood of people who had received many blood transfusions. When a person receives blood from someone else, there are foreign proteins in the blood. Some of these proteins might prompt the body to build antibodies. The researchers could examine these antibodies to figure out what the foreign proteins were.

In 1963 at the Institute for Cancer Research at Fox Chase Center in Philadelphia, Dr. Blumberg, working with Dr. Harvey Alter at the National Institutes of Health (NIH), discovered a set of antibodies in a New York hemophiliac's blood that reacted with the blood of an Australian aboriginal. That meant that there must be an antigen (a foreign protein) in the blood of the aboriginal that prompted antibody production. Dr. Blumberg called the protein the Au antigen, for Australia.

Drs. Blumberg and Alter tested the blood of people from different areas around the world to see whether the antigen was present in other populations, too. Although the protein was very rare in the United States, it was more common in blood samples of people from some parts of Africa and from parts of Asia such as the Philippines. Then they found that blood samples from leukemia patients at the University of Pennsylvania's medical center often contained the Au protein.

The researchers wondered whether the protein might be an indicator of people who were prone to this type of cancer. They decided to examine the blood of a group of children with Down's syndrome, because these children are 20 to 2000 times more likely to develop leukemia than other children. They found that 30 percent of the Down's syndrome patients in a nearby institution were positive for Au antigen. "Until this time all the individuals with Au who had been identified either lived in Australia or some other distant place or were sick with leukemia," Dr. Blumberg says.[4] The researchers wondered what patients with Down's syndrome and leukemia could have in common with an Australian aboriginal.

The mystery began to unravel when James, one of the teenagers with Down's syndrome who had previously tested negative for Au, suddenly tested positive. Tests revealed that James had recently developed hepatitis. It seemed likely that the Au antigen had something to do with hepatitis. Now things started to make sense. Hemophiliacs and leukemia patients receive numerous blood transfusions, and people with Down's syndrome have weakened immune systems—perfect conditions for contracting hepatitis. And the disease is common in Asia and Africa, which would explain why the Au antigen turned up more frequently there.

In 1966 Dr. Barbara Werner, who had been testing Au samples in the lab, felt ill and tested herself for the Au protein.

Sure enough, her blood tested positive. She became the first person to be diagnosed using the Au test.[5]

Saul Krugman sent samples of the MS-I and MS-2 hepatitis-infected blood to Dr. Blumberg to see if they contained the Australia antigen. It was not present in the MS-I sample, but it was present in the MS-2, or hepatitis B strain.

Dr. Blumberg hadn't identified a hepatitis virus, but he discovered the next best thing—a marker to detect hepatitis B. His work helped to confirm Dr. Krugman's discovery that there were two different hepatitis strains, and in turn Dr. Krugman's studies helped scientists understand the significance of the Au antigen. The World Health Organization called Dr. Blumberg's discovery, "the most spectacular advance in the seemingly insoluble problem of human hepatitis."[6] Baruch Blumberg won a Nobel Prize for Medicine in 1976 for his discovery of the Au antigen. His discovery opened up the way for the development of a vaccine that would prevent infection and spread of the virus.

Practical Applications to Save Lives

Dr. Blumberg's lab began to reject all Au-positive blood in their studies, and the number of patients who developed hepatitis after transfusions fell by two-thirds. Within a year other hospitals were rejecting HBV-infected blood donations. A *New York Times* article in July 1970 helped the rest of the medical community to accept the findings. The article said that the virus that causes hepatitis had been found, and that it

Dr. Baruch Blumberg won the Nobel Prize for Medicine in 1976 for his discovery of the Au antigen. His work was called "the most spectacular advance in the seemingly insoluble problem of human hepatitis" by the World Health Organization.

was being spread through blood transfusions. As the discovery became more widely known, several lawsuits were filed against hospitals by patients who had contracted hepatitis after being hospitalized. It wasn't long before many states required blood to be tested for the Au protein. Since the early 1970s the American Association of Blood Banks has required all donor blood to be Au-tested.[7]

Eventually the Au protein was found to be a protein on the outer surface of the HBV virus. Fifteen years after Au was discovered, the hepatitis B virus was seen under an electron microscope. But it wasn't until 1986 that scientists were able to grow the virus in a test tube.

Tracking Down Other Hepatitis Viruses

The hepatitis A virus that was present in Dr. Krugman's MS-1 sample was found in 1975 by Drs. Stephen Feinstone, Robert Purcell, and Albert Kapikian at the NIH. Then they were able to devise a blood test to detect it. Since blood from donors was already being tested for hepatitis B virus and some people were still developing hepatitis after transfusions, the researchers thought these people must be getting hepatitis A. They took their blood test to Dr. Harvey Alter, who had been studying the blood of surgery patients. To their surprise, none of the patients who had developed hepatitis after transfusions were infected with hepatitis A. Something else must be causing these hepatitis cases! The researchers were unable to identify the cause, which they suspected was another virus, so they named the illness "non-A, non-B hepatitis." In

1987 Michael Houghton and colleagues at Chiron Corporation in California identified the virus that seemed to be causing most of the cases of non-A, non-B hepatitis—and it was named hepatitis C, or HCV.

The Delta Factor

A young Italian doctor named Mario Rizzetto saw an unusual protein in the blood of a patient with hepatitis B "that didn't make sense."[8] But European scientists didn't pay much attention, because many researchers were claiming they'd found something involved with hepatitis. Dr. Rizzetto wrote to Robert Purcell at the National Institutes of Health, hoping to pursue his research with American hepatitis investigators. Dr. Purcell hooked Dr. Rizzetto up with John Gerin, head of the division of molecular biology and immunology at Georgetown University's research station in Maryland.

The Italian doctor traveled to Maryland and worked with Gerin's team to try to isolate the strange protein. "To get that antigen out of that liver took almost nine months. It's a very unusual protein," says Dr. Gerin.[9]

Researchers at Georgetown University, working with Mario Rizzetto's protein, found that when HBV-infected chimpanzees were infected with this new protein they suddenly developed a severe case of hepatitis. (HBV doesn't normally cause as serious a disease in chimpanzees as it does in humans.) Oddly enough, when the chimps were infected with the new agent, the markers that indicated all HBV infection seemed to go away.

In 1977 the researchers identified the virus and found that it was unlike any other virus that was known to infect humans. It was, in fact, more like a plant virus than a human virus. And it seemed to cause the most severe type of hepatitis. The researchers called it the delta agent or delta particle, and the disease associated with it was named hepatitis D. They found that the delta particle was able to infect a wide range of animal species, which is unusual for a virus. However, a person can become infected only when HBV is present.

Hepatitis E

In 1988 researcher Daniel W. Bradley of the Centers for Disease Control, working with Genelabs in Redwood City, California, discovered another hepatitis virus called epidemic non-A, non-B, or hepatitis E. Like hepatitis A, it is usually transmitted through water that is contaminated by sewage. It is rare in the United States but has caused many epidemics in Africa and Asia.

3

What Is Hepatitis?

Kathy, a twenty-three-year-old New York secretary, developed hepatitis three and a half months after getting her ears pierced at a jewelry store. At first she had flulike symptoms. Her back ached, and she felt extremely tired. Then her urine turned dark brown, and the whites of her eyes and her skin turned yellow. She was hospitalized a few days later. Despite doctors' efforts to help her, she went into a coma and died.[1]

Gino, a twenty-nine-year-old business person in New York City, ate raw oysters that he had bought from a street vendor. Several weeks later, he began to feel ill. He had no appetite and noticed that his urine seemed rather dark. Soon his skin and the whites of his eyes turned yellowish. But the illness was mild. Gino lost only one day's work, and within a few weeks he was feeling normal again. "I was definitely lucky," he says. "It could have been a lot worse."[2]

Joan, a fifty-seven-year-old secretary, was not as lucky. She had periodic bouts of what seemed like the flu; she was tired, and she was bothered by a sore throat, aching joints, and tender glands. She would take off from work for a few days each time it occurred, but the attacks seemed to get worse. Then one day at work in 1988, she lay down to rest for a moment but couldn't get up. "My doctor said, 'Go home and stay in bed for a couple of weeks.' I thought, 'Two weeks' rest and I'll be raring to go.' But I'm still home four years later."[3]

Hepato is Greek for "liver," and *itis* means "inflammation." The different types of hepatitis are caused by different things, but they all produce inflammation of the liver. Usually there is swelling and tenderness. Most people with hepatitis recover completely. Rarely, the disease will be so severe that the patient dies of liver failure (for example, Kathy, who was infected while getting her ears pierced). More often, when death occurs because of hepatitis, the liver has been severely damaged over a long period of time, and serious liver diseases developed many years later.

What Causes Hepatitis

Toxic Hepatitis. Hepatitis can be caused by viruses or by liver damage due to toxic substances. Toxic hepatitis is a deterioration of the liver cells caused by chemicals, alcohol, drugs, and industrial compounds. Alcohol abuse is a common cause of toxic liver damage. Volatile compounds that contaminate the

THE AMAZING LIVER

The liver is the largest organ in the body, and one of the most important. It is found in the upper right side of the abdomen, in front of the stomach.

The liver has more than five hundred different vital functions. It manufactures bile needed for digesting fats, and it stores carbohydrates to use as fuel for muscles. It produces the fatlike substance cholesterol that the body needs to build cell membranes, as well as proteins that help blood to clot normally to prevent excessive bleeding. The liver regulates hormones that control growth and sex. It helps to detoxify harmful substances that get into the bloodstream. Many vitamins and minerals, such as vitamins A and D, iron, and copper, are stored in the liver until they are needed.

The liver can take a lot of abuse. It will continue to carry out its many jobs after as much as two-thirds of it is damaged. (It can even grow back to normal size if up to as much as 70 percent is removed; the skin and mucous membranes are the only other parts of the body that can regenerate like that.) But when the liver becomes too damaged to function, a person will die—we cannot live without a liver.

air in certain workplaces can also cause hepatitis. A chemical called carbon tetrachloride, for example, was once widely used in dry cleaning until its damaging effect on the liver was discovered. Medications such as acetaminophen (the popular pain reliever commonly sold as Tylenol™), disulfiram (used in the treatment of alcoholism), and isoniazid (a drug used to treat tuberculosis) can cause liver inflammation when taken in large amounts or over a long period of time. Some "natural" substances can damage the liver, too. Several herbal remedies—including chaparral, an evergreen shrub found in some herbal teas; comfrey, a hairy-leafed plant used as an aid to digestion; and an herb in the mint family called germander, whose blossoms are used in teas, tonics, and herbal capsules for losing weight—have been found to cause toxic hepatitis in some people.

Viral Hepatitis. There are several contagious diseases that attack the liver. Viral hepatitis, caused by at least five different viruses, is the most common. These viruses—hepatitis A virus (HAV), hepatitis B virus (HBV), hepatitis C virus (HCV), delta hepatitis (HDV), and hepatitis E (HEV)—are very different, but they all attack liver cells as their primary target.

Hepatitis A used to be called infectious hepatitis. The virus is a tiny sphere, 27 nanometers (less than a millionth of an inch) wide. Inside an outer coat of protein it contains a single strand of RNA, a chemical containing the virus's genes: the complete blueprint for producing new virus particles, in coded form. Scientists believe it belongs to the same family as the polio virus. Hepatitis A virus is fairly heat resistant—it can

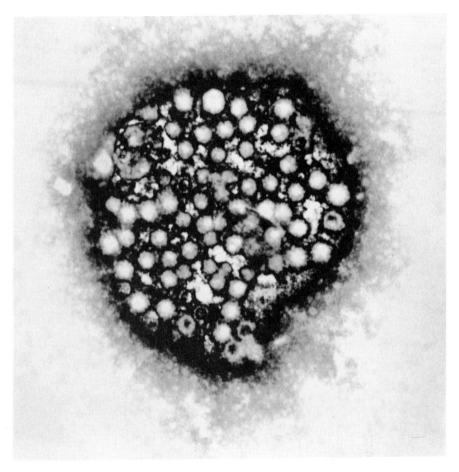

The hepatitis A virus (shown here, greatly magnified) is spherical in shape and has an outer shell of protein which encases a single strand of RNA.

withstand 60°C (140°F) for 30 minutes—but treatment of contaminated food or water in a microwave oven can prevent transmission.

Hepatitis B used to be called serum hepatitis. At first scientists didn't know what the Australia (Au) antigen was. They saw many small particles (about 20 nm) when blood samples of hepatitis patients were observed under an electron microscope. Some of these particles were round, and some were shaped like sausages. Were these the virus or only part of the virus? In 1970, an English scientist named D. M. S. Dane identified the hepatitis B virus. It was a small, spherical virus with a double-walled protein coat, but it was about 40 nm and thus was twice the size of the particles that had originally been identified under the electron microscope. The virus and the particles both contained the Australia antigen, so both caused the body to produce antibodies. But the virus contains the genetic material, an incomplete double ring of DNA and enzymes. The smaller particles do not contain the genetic material that the virus needs to reproduce, but there are as many as ten thousand times more of them than of the virus. (The sausage-shaped particles are clumps of virus coat protein.)

The reason why hepatitis B is so infectious was quite clear from the microscopic studies—there were as many as 100 million particles of infectious hepatitis B virus per milliliter of infected blood (a teaspoon contains 5 milliliters). By contrast, there are only one or two particles of the AIDS virus in a milliliter of infected blood. Some scientists think that

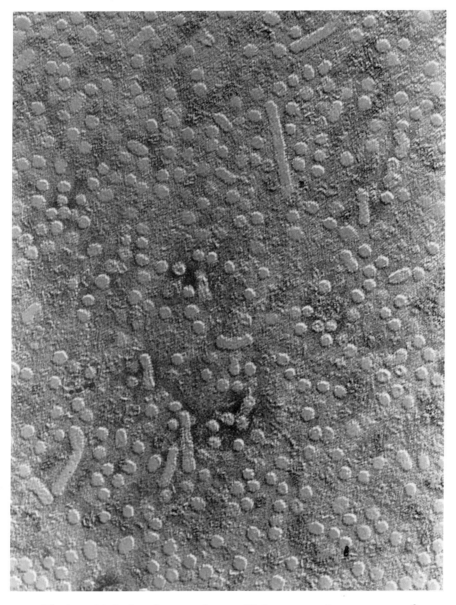

The hepatitis B virus, here greatly magnified, appears to have two types of particles. Some are round and some are sausage-shaped.

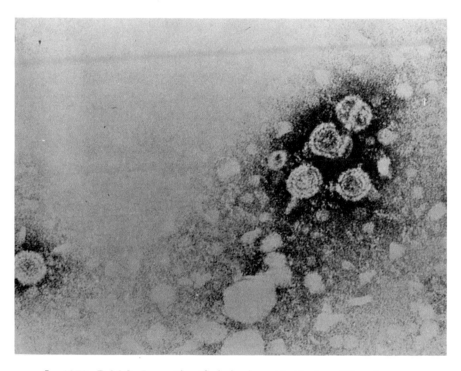

In 1970, D.M.S. Dane identified the hepatitis B virus. The virus was actually twice the size of particles that were originally thought to be hepatitis B particles. Above is the hepatitis B virus with Dane particles.

hepatitis B virus is related to retroviruses like the HIV virus that causes AIDS.

Hepatitis C used to be called non-A, non-B hepatitis. The virus contains a small single strand of RNA. It belongs to a group called togaviruses, which also includes the viruses that cause rubella and yellow fever. Hepatitis C particles are present in much smaller amounts than hepatitis B. There are only 100 particles per milliliter.

Hepatitis D, sometimes called delta hepatitis, is a single strand of RNA, 35 to 37 nm in diameter, coated with hepatitis B antigen. Hepatitis D is not a complete virus because it cannot reproduce. It can infect only cells that are already infected with the hepatitis B virus. Normally, a virus can enter a cell because a protein on its outer coat matches up with a receptor site on the surface of a cell, like a key fitting into a lock. But hepatitis D is just bare genetic material without an outer coat. It steals the hepatitis B outer coat so that it can enter at the same receptor site. Delta forces the cell to produce mostly delta RNA and then takes the hepatitis B coats that have been produced. "It's the cuckoo of the viral kingdom, stealing the coat of the B virus just as the cuckoo steals the nests of other birds," says Michael Houghton at Chiron Corporation in California.[4] Dr. Houghton believes that there are other agents out there that work the way delta does to make diseases worse.

Scientists wonder where delta came from. They believe that it is like more primitive plant viruses called viroids. Like delta, viroids are made up of a naked RNA that can't make its own outer coat. Viruses usually contain enzymes in addition to genetic material. The enzymes help the virus convince the host cell to manufacture virus parts instead of host cell parts. But delta contains no enzymes. Scientists aren't sure exactly how it reproduces. Perhaps it borrows the infected cell's enzymes.

Hepatitis E used to be called enteric (meaning passed from feces) or epidemic non-A, non-B hepatitis. It is an RNA virus, 32 nm wide. Some researchers think hepatitis E is a new virus that is only between fifty and seventy-five years old.

There may also be at least one other non-A, non-B hepatitis virus that causes a small number of hepatitis cases after transfusions. Other viruses—particularly herpes viruses such as the Epstein-Barr virus (which causes infectious mononucleosis), cytomegalovirus (also causing mono), chicken pox, and cold sore viruses—can affect the liver and cause hepatitis. Liver inflammation can also be caused by the yellow fever virus and congenital rubella virus. Conditions that mimic viral hepatitis include Wilson's disease, severe congestive heart failure, and mushroom poisoning.

What Happens in the Body

The hepatitis A and E viruses first enter the gut and begin reproducing. They spread to the liver and multiply in liver cells. Hepatitis B, C, and D enter the bloodstream; when they pass through the liver, they enter liver cells and begin to reproduce. The body attacks the infected cells, which causes the liver to become inflamed. "The usual aftermath of hepatitis B infection is that the liver repairs itself, leaving antibodies to the surface antigen as a sign that infection has occurred and the body has defeated it," says Dr. Eugene R. Schiff, a liver expert at the University of Miami School of Medicine.[5]

The incubation period (the amount of time that elapses between infection and the development of symptoms) varies for the different hepatitis viruses. Hepatitis A and E may develop as few as two weeks after exposure, but usually appear after four weeks. For hepatitis B and C it may take up to six months before symptoms develop. (The average incubation period is two to three months for hepatitis B and six to nine weeks for hepatitis C.) In experiments on chimpanzees, hepatitis D developed two to ten weeks after infection.

Hepatitis Symptoms

All five forms of hepatitis often produce similar symptoms. These symptoms can begin suddenly or develop gradually. Infants and young children often have no symptoms at all. Hepatitis A is usually a mild disease; the few deaths that occur are usually among older people who already had liver problems. Hepatitis B can be mild to severe; hepatitis C is generally mild; and delta hepatitis has the potential to be severe. Hepatitis E is not usually severe, except in pregnant women.

Early signs of hepatitis may include flulike symptoms such as fatigue, low-grade fever, headache, loss of appetite, nausea, vomiting, and stiff or aching joints.

After three to seven days, skin rash and pain in the liver might develop. The urine may become dark brown and foamy, and the feces may be pale. The person may develop jaundice, in which the skin and whites of the eyes become yellowish. The color is due to a chemical called bilirubin, which is produced in the liver when old red blood cells are broken down. This reddish-brown pigment normally is part of bile, the liver secretion that aids fat digestion. But liver inflammation blocks the flow of bile to the gallbladder. The damaged liver cannot filter bilirubin out of the blood properly, so this pigment builds up in the blood and tissues and gives the skin the characteristic yellowish color. Bilirubin also produces the dark color of the urine; the feces are light in color because liver blockage prevents normal elimination of the pigment through the bowels.

After two to eight weeks of bed rest, most people feel better, although fatigue may continue for a few more weeks. In older people, symptoms may last for several months. Symptoms may recur before the person is completely cured. When hepatitis clears up within six months, it is called acute hepatitis.

In very rare cases hepatitis symptoms develop quickly and become very severe. This less common form of hepatitis is called fulminant hepatitis or fast-progressing hepatitis, and it requires prompt medical attention—it can be fatal in up to 70 to 80 percent of cases. The kidneys may fail, and the liver shrinks as cells are killed. The person may fall into a coma and die.

Some people infected with hepatitis B or C may develop chronic hepatitis because the immune system cannot get rid of the virus. The person becomes a carrier who can continue to infect people for the rest of his or her life. Half of chronic hepatitis carriers feel no symptoms, although the liver may continue to be inflamed. In chronic persistent hepatitis the inflammation isn't serious, and the liver can return to normal by itself after a few years. The person is then healthy but is still a carrier. The liver inflammation can also progress to a more severe form, however.

When the inflammation is more severe it is called chronic active hepatitis. Country singer Naomi Judd suffers from a debilitating case of chronic active hepatitis C. People with chronic active hepatitis may lose weight, feel tired, have abdominal pain and jaundice, and may develop scarring of the liver (called cirrhosis) and liver failure. One out of five people with severe chronic active hepatitis also develop problems in the eyes, joints, kidneys, thyroid, large intestines, or skin. Unlike chronic persistent hepatitis, this form rarely gets better on its own. People with either type of chronic hepatitis have a greater risk of developing liver cancer or other serious liver damage fifteen to fifty years later. The risk of chronic carriers of HBV developing cancer, for example, is 100 times higher than normal.[6]

From 5 to 10 percent of American adults who have hepatitis B develop a lifelong infection; it is estimated that up to one and a half million Americans currently have chronic hepatitis B virus infections. In other parts of the world the chances of becoming a carrier are even greater. In Africa and Asia one person in five is a chronic carrier, and southern European and Mediterranean countries have a high incidence of carriers, too. (In southeast Asia and tropical Africa chronic carriers represent 10 percent of the population, but they are only one percent in populations of North America and most of western Europe.) About three-quarters of the estimated 200 to 300 million HBV carriers live in Asia.[7]

When HBV causes fulminant hepatitis, the problem is not a stronger form of the virus, but a stronger immune response by the host. The chronic state seems to be related to a weak immune response, which would explain why infants, who have immature immune systems, are so much more likely to become carriers. (Up to 90 percent of children who are infected at birth become carriers, and 30 to 60 percent of infected children under five develop chronic hepatitis B.) High levels of virus remain in the body, but antibodies are not produced.

People who are infected with hepatitis C have an even greater chance of becoming chronic carriers. At first doctors believed that an alarming two-thirds of these patients can become carriers, but a recent study has found that nearly everyone who becomes infected with hepatitis C will go on to become a chronic carrier.[8] All together, there are an estimated 2 to 5 million Americans who are chronic carriers of HCV. Delta infection can also be chronic. When a person with chronic hepatitis B becomes infected by delta, the result is usually a more severe form of the disease. Hepatitis A and hepatitis E, on the other hand, are acute liver infections. There are no chronic hepatitis A or E carriers.

Complications of Hepatitis

Most people who develop hepatitis B recover completely. In rare cases, acute yellow atrophy (massive liver damage, referred to as necrosis) can lead to liver failure, coma, and death. (Fulminant hepatitis develops in about 0.1 percent of hepatitis A patients, and many die.) But more than 6,500 Americans die annually of chronic hepatitis B, 5,000 die of cirrhosis of the liver caused by hepatitis B, and 1,500 die from HBV-related liver cancer. Another 8,000 to 10,000 die each year from HCV-related liver problems.[9]

For years doctors have suspected that hepatitis B was one of the most common causes of liver cancer in the world. But, as Dr. Ira Jacobson, a hepatitis expert at New York Hospital–Cornell Medical Center, notes, "We are coming to recognize in this country that liver cancer may more commonly arise from hepatitis C than from hepatitis B."[10] Between 25 and 40 percent of babies who become HBV or HCV carriers will die of liver disease, cirrhosis, or liver cancer.

When the study claiming that most people infected with hepatitis C would become chronic carriers was released, doctors were worried that this would mean that even more would die of liver problems than had previously been thought. However, the study, which examined the lives of patients who had been infected with hepatitis C, also had a positive side. Jules Dienstag, a hepatitis expert at Massachusetts General Hospital in Boston, points out that "until now we presumed that anyone with cirrhosis and hepatitis C had a good chance of going downhill. But in fact, there is a population of people who do fairly well. We all feel this is encouraging."[11]

Becoming infected with both delta and hepatitis B at the same time increases the chances that severe fulminant hepatitis will develop. (In fact, health experts now believe that such dual infections are responsible for up to half of all cases of fulminant hepatitis that were previously blamed on hepatitis B.) These cases are also more likely to be fatal; from 2 to 20 percent of the double-infected patients die, compared to only one percent of those with hepatitis B.

If hepatitis D is caught after a person has already been infected with the B virus, chronic hepatitis usually develops, and the liver damage is usually worse. From 70 to 80 percent of such patients develop cirrhosis of the liver, as opposed to 15 to 30 percent of patients with chronic HBV alone.

Researchers believe that one reason why the immune system is greatly weakened in people with chronic hepatitis is that antibodies against the delta particle also attack cells of the thymus gland. The thymus normally "trains" special disease-fighting white blood cells called T cells. Thymus damage may explain why the body doesn't mount much of a fight against the chronic virus infection. This is similar to what happens in AIDS patients.

Who Gets Hepatitis?

People of all ages, all around the world, can get hepatitis. In the United States, 40 percent of hepatitis cases are caused by hepatitis A; 40 percent by HBV (or HBV with delta); and 20 percent by HCV.

Hepatitis A infects about 150,000 Americans each year. By adulthood 30 to 70 percent of Americans have been exposed to hepatitis A with little or no symptoms; "it's a very common childhood sub-clinical infection," says Dr. Harvey Alter of the NIH.[12] In developing nations, almost everyone is exposed to the virus in childhood. When adults from industrialized nations visit these countries, they are susceptible and can get this disease from contaminated water or foods. Their symptoms are usually much worse than those in children, as is typical of many viral diseases.

High-risk groups in the United States are the children and staff at day-care centers, residents of institutions for the intellectually handicapped, prison inmates, male homosexuals, sanitation workers, and handlers of primates. (Hepatitis A also infects chimpanzees and a few other primates such as marmosets.) Major outbreaks may occur in countries where the sanitation conditions have greatly improved over the years but the virus is still present, such as the Mediterranean basin, the Middle East, and parts of Asia. Under these conditions, adults may have escaped childhood infection because of better sanitation conditions, so they are not immune.

Hepatitis B is a growing problem. According to the Centers for Disease Control (CDC), there was a 30 percent

Looking downstream towards St. Peter's Basilica and the Ponte Sant'Angelo, the Tiber River may look picturesque, but scientists have recently discovered the hepatitis A virus in its waters and Romans are calling the river "an open-air sewer."

increase in HBV cases between 1979 and 1989. Each year about 300,000 Americans get hepatitis B, and it is estimated that one out of twenty people in the United States will get hepatitis B sometime during their lives. The rate is much higher in other places around the world. In sub-Saharan Africa, for example, 70 to 90 percent of adults have been infected with hepatitis B.[13]

Half of the 300,000 Americans infected with HBV become acutely ill, and 300 of them die. The other half have no symptoms, or the illness is so mild they don't notice it or mistake it for a simple cold.

In the Third World, most people get the virus when it is transmitted from an infected mother to her child. So hepatitis B is mostly a disease of infants in developing nations. But in the United States and other Western countries, most reported cases of hepatitis B occur in young adults. "From age 20 to 29 is the peak risk period, especially because of sexual activity, lifestyle, and possible experimentation with drugs. Children—except the offspring of carrier mothers—are not at high risk," says Dr. Robert J. Gerety, executive director of virus and cell biology research at Merck Sharp & Dohme Research Laboratories.[14] Males get hepatitis B much more often than females. When exposed to the virus, male adults have a 70 percent chance of coming down with the disease, while women develop symptoms only 33 percent of the time.

During the 1960s, 35 percent of the people who received more than one unit of blood during surgery developed hepatitis B. (For that reason it was called serum hepatitis

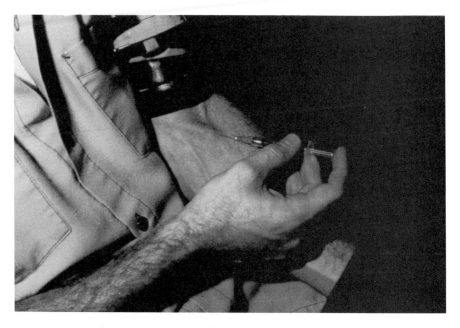

Intravenous drug users are among those at high risk of contracting hepatitis B.

then.) Today, because of blood screening, only one percent of HBV cases are related to transfusions.[15] Hepatitis B occurs mainly in people at high risk, such as IV drug users, male homosexuals, heterosexuals with several partners, health-care workers who are exposed to blood, infants who are born to infected mothers, and immigrants from areas such as Africa, China, and Southeast Asia.

The hepatitis B virus is similar to the hepadnaviruses that infect woodchucks, squirrels, Peking ducks, herons, and snakes. But the only other animals that are known to be infected by HBV are primates such as the chimpanzee and gibbon.

Hepatitis C is believed to cause between 150,000 and 250,000 new cases in the United States each year. Hemophiliacs and drug abusers are at the greatest risk. Dr. Miriam Alter of the CDC has found that the most common link among the other cases is poverty. Researchers have found that many people infected with hepatitis C don't even know it. Ever since doctors were given a blood test to detect hepatitis C in their patients, they have been turning up more and more sufferers who have no symptoms. From 20 to 40 percent of patients in inner-city hospitals are infected, as are 80 percent of drug users. Dr. Leonard B. Seeff of the Veterans Affairs Hospital in Washington has found that 40 percent of his patients had hepatitis C, although most didn't realize it. "I believe that hepatitis C is a tremendously common disease and that we have not known about it. We are seeing the tip of an iceberg," he says.[16]

There is some evidence to indicate that HCV may be a relatively new virus. At the very least, it was not as common in the past as it is today. Scientists suspect that the increase in intravenous drug abuse has caused the number of cases to skyrocket. And the fact that most of those who are infected become chronic carriers constantly increases the pool of people who can continue to spread the disease.

Hepatitis D affects about 15 million people worldwide. Delta hepatitis is endemic in Italy and other places in the Mediterranean and in several places in South America, including northern Colombia. In the United States it is mostly found in IV drug users and male homosexuals.

Hepatitis E is not a problem in the United States. It has

A NEW EPIDEMIC?

Doctors tested stored blood samples of World War II soldiers who either had or had not been vaccinated with the contaminated yellow fever vaccine. Up to one percent of the soldiers who were vaccinated became chronic carriers of hepatitis B. But Veterans Affairs Hospital researcher Dr. Leonard Seeff found no blood samples of either vaccinated or unvaccinated soldiers that gave a positive reaction for HCV. Dr. Seeff believes that HCV existed back in the forties, but just wasn't common.[17]

been reported in Asia (especially India), Africa, Mexico, and Russia, and it has caused at least twenty widespread epidemics in seventeen countries. Travelers may become infected and spread it when they return home. Most people recover completely, except pregnant women—one in five pregnant women with hepatitis E can die of fulminant liver failure.[18]

4

How Hepatitis Is Spread

n 1944, 350 children at a Pennsylvania summer camp developed hepatitis. Investigators poured vegetable dyes into the toilets and found that the drinking water soon became tinted—sewage was leaking into the drinking wells. In 1956, 30,000 people developed hepatitis A when an overflowing sewer polluted drinking water in Delhi, India.[1] In Shanghai, 300,000 people developed hepatitis A after eating contaminated raw clams in 1988.[2]

A group of New York City eighth graders on a field trip discovered many broken vials of blood that had washed ashore onto a public beach. When the vials were tested, some of them were found to be contaminated with hepatitis B virus. They had been dumped by the owner of a blood-testing lab into a nearby waterway.[3]

A young man was mugged in New York's Central Park. He lost his wallet and his watch, and the mugger scratched him with a knife. He felt lucky he hadn't been killed. But six months later he developed hepatitis B—the mugger's knife had been contaminated.[4]

How Hepatitis A and E Are Spread

Hepatitis viruses are spread in different ways. Hepatitis A and E are shed in feces. A person can be affected through direct contact with feces, such as when changing an infected baby's diaper. Outbreaks are sometimes associated with day care centers. Children often have no symptoms, but they can carry the infection home to their families. "You get a lot of young children fond of mouthing everything. There's a lot of diaper changing, and the virus can easily spread to many children, who take it home to their siblings and parents," says Dr. David Nalin, director of clinical research for infectious diseases at Merck Research Laboratories in Blue Bell, Pennsylvania.[5] Having anal sex with an infected partner can also spread the disease.

Indirect contamination is more often the cause. Poor sanitation conditions may allow feces to contaminate the water supply or food. Many outbreaks of hepatitis A have developed when people ate raw shellfish (especially oysters) grown in sewage-polluted water. Eating food handled by an infected person who hasn't washed his or her hands properly after going to the bathroom, or using contaminated eating utensils can spread hepatitis A. That's what happened in

Montana and Georgia, when fifty-seven people developed hepatitis A after eating frozen strawberries that were probably picked by a migrant worker infected with HAV.[6] (The CDC points out, however, that this type of transmission is very rare in the United States.) If you touch a contaminated surface in a public restroom or on a train or bus, and then put your hands in your mouth you can also become infected.[7]

Hepatitis E, like hepatitis A, is spread mainly by polluted water or food contaminated by it.

Hepatitis B: More Infectious Than AIDS

When Lisa's doctor told her she had hepatitis B, she was very surprised. She had never taken intravenous drugs. She had never had a blood transfusion, and she had not had multiple sex partners. Those were the ways the doctor told her many people are infected. So, how had she caught hepatitis? At an American Hepatitis Association support group, another hepatitis sufferer mentioned that she wasn't going back to a particular nail salon because the manicurist often nicked her. Lisa went to the same manicurist, and the two women realized that that's how they must both have been infected.[8]

A team of Swedish runners were running a cross-country race that took them through branches and underbrush, causing minor scratches on their legs. After the race they shared several towels. A few months later, many of the team members came down with hepatitis B—they had been infected from blood on the towels.[9]

Two dozen patients with diabetes in one hospital ward

developed hepatitis B after using the same fingerstick device to test their blood sugar levels.[10]

Nick, a hospital security guard, was on duty when a car pulled up to the hospital steps and dropped off a gunshot victim. Nick quickly helped the bleeding man into the emergency room, never dreaming that a few months later he would be a patient in the hospital, suffering from hepatitis B.[11]

Hepatitis B virus can be found in blood and body fluids such as semen, tears, and saliva. A person who comes in contact with even small amounts of infected blood could be infected if the virus gets into his or her bloodstream through a cut in the skin or mucous membranes. Hepatitis B is spread in the same way as AIDS but it is fifteen times more common than AIDS, and a hundred times more contagious. "If you got stuck with a needle from someone with AIDS, you'd have half a percent chance of contracting the virus, but with hepatitis B, your chances would be as high as thirty percent," says Dr. Jerome Boscia, director of vaccine development for SmithKline Beecham.[12]

Like AIDS, hepatitis B can be spread through contact with infected blood, such as by sharing infected needles. It may also be spread from mothers who are carriers to their children at birth or soon after birth. When a firefighter or rescue worker performs CPR on a person with hepatitis who is bleeding, or when a police officer wrestles with an infected crime suspect, they have been exposed to hepatitis. According to the CDC, 55 percent of hepatitis B is acquired through

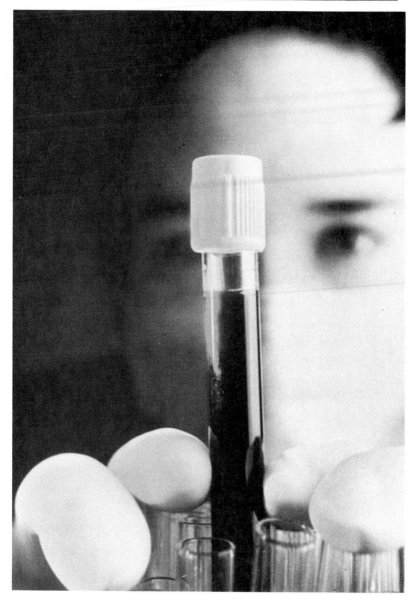

Hepatitis B can be found in blood and other body fluids. Just a small amount of contaminated blood is enough to infect a person if it gets into his or her bloodstream.

sexual contact (including 41 percent heterosexual activity and 14 percent homosexual activity), 12 percent through sharing needles by drug abusers, 4 percent by household contact, 2 percent among health-care workers, and one percent in other ways; how the other 26 percent develop hepatitis B is unknown.[13]

A person might not even realize that he or she is coming in contact with infected blood. It is reported that the virus can survive on a dry surface for a week or longer.[14] The American Liver Foundation warns that hepatitis B can be transmitted by puncturing the skin with instruments used in dental and medical procedures, as well as from a barber's razor and instruments used in acupuncture, tattooing, ear piercing, and

THE MOTHER-CHILD CONNECTION

"Women who are chronic carriers are almost always unaware of it. They have no symptoms," says Dr. Cladd Stevens, head of the epidemiology laboratory at the New York Blood Center.[15] Worldwide, the passage of hepatitis by chronic carrier mothers to their children is the most important link leading to liver damage. "The babies may not have a problem for fifteen or twenty-five years, but, worldwide, more people will die of hepatitis B than of AIDS," says Dr. Saul Krugman at New York University Medical Center.[16]

manicures. In kidney dialysis, for example, needles are inserted in the patient's veins and his or her blood flows out through tubes into a machine. There it is cleared of poisonous wastes and then returned to the patient's veins. This may be done several times a week—with plenty of opportunity for contamination that could spread the disease to other patients or the medical staff.

"But the most effective means of transmission is sexual contact other than kissing," says Dr. Ira S. Goldman at North Shore University Hospital–Cornell University Medical College in Manhasset, New York. "The scary thing is that a lot of people don't know they have it. They may be asymptomatic and transmit it through intercourse."[17] Doctors

 SPECIAL CONCERN FOR HEALTH-CARE WORKERS

Charles, a dentist, recovered from hepatitis B only to find out he was a chronic carrier. To avoid infecting his patients, he wore double gloves at all times. Later two of his patients developed hepatitis. They might not have gotten it from him, but he decided to give up his practice.[18]

With the fear of AIDS, many people are worried about going to the doctor or dentist. This worry is largely misplaced. "Doctors and dentists, who are exposed to the blood and mouth fluids of many patients, are much more at risk than their patients," comments Dr. Ira Goldman at North Shore University Hospital–Cornell University Medical College.[19]

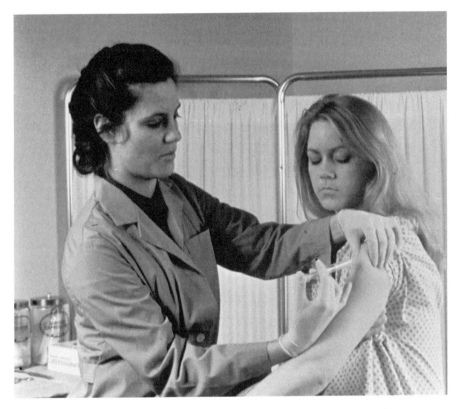

Although many people are reluctant to visit their doctors or dentists because of fear of getting AIDS or hepatitis, health care workers, who are exposed to their patients' blood, are at higher risk than their patients.

are worried about sexually active teenagers who may not be aware of the risk of developing hepatitis B through sexual contact.

Although the cause of many cases is unknown, "I think many people whose infections can't be traced are getting it either sexually or through living in a household with a carrier who hasn't been identified," says Dr. Miriam Alter, chief of the epidemiology section of the hepatitis branch of the CDC. "All you need is a minute amount of blood getting into your bloodstream, say by brushing your teeth with an infected person's brush or using the same razor."[20]

Hepatitis C and D: Blood-Borne Hepatitis

Hepatitis C is spread mainly through contaminated needles and blood transfusions with contaminated blood. Since scientists came up with blood tests to detect contaminated blood, the number of cases of hepatitis C contracted after transfusions has been greatly reduced. According to the CDC, 2 percent of infections with HCV are from transfusions (down from 7 to 12 percent before tests were available), 5 percent from occupational exposure, and 40 percent from sharing needles by IV drug users; the causes of 35 to 40 percent of the cases are unknown.[21]

Doctors had thought that sexual contact was not a big factor in the spread of hepatitis C, because there is evidence that it does not spread easily through sexual activity. (Very few spouses develop the disease, for example.) But a study published in 1993 suggests that because of the large number

WILL <u>YOU</u> GET HEPATITIS?

You may be at risk for hepatitis if you:[22]

- have a job that exposes you to human blood (health-care workers, police, firefighters).

- live in the same house with someone who has a lifelong hepatitis virus infection.

- inject drugs.

- have sex with a person infected with hepatitis B, C, D, or E virus.

- have sex with more than one partner.

- are a child whose parents were born in Southeast Asia, Africa, the Amazon Basin in South America, the Pacific Islands, or the Middle East.

- are a patient or work in an institution for the developmentally disabled.

- have hemophilia.

- travel internationally to areas with a high prevalence of hepatitis.

of chronic carriers in the country, "sexual behavior could nonetheless transmit a significant portion of new infections in the United States annually."[23]

Hepatitis B and C spread through blood, so since many people bleed while brushing their teeth or shaving, using the toothbrush or razor of an infected person could spread the disease. Kissing might also spread these infections if cuts are present in the mouth or lips. Some scientists suspect that mosquitoes and other blood-sucking insects may also be spreading these forms of hepatitis, although at this point this is just speculation.[24]

Hepatitis D is spread through sexual contact and infected needles. (Remember that HDV can infect only people who are infected with HBV.)

Can You Get Hepatitis More Than Once?

Once you completely recover from a particular type of viral hepatitis you can't get it again, although in some people the condition becomes chronic and can last their whole lives. But since there are at least five different viruses that cause hepatitis, you can get one of the others (though not D if you are immune to B). Becoming infected with B and C at the same time may actually cause a much more severe, dangerous case of hepatitis. A person who has recovered from a case of viral hepatitis could also develop hepatitis again due to other causes, such as alcohol or other drugs.

5

Diagnosing Hepatitis

Diane, a twenty-seven-year-old, had a knot in her side that soon became a burning pain that wouldn't go away. She felt exhausted all the time, didn't feel like eating, and lost five pounds. After two weeks her urine turned dark brown, and she knew something was wrong. She went to her doctor, but he said it was just a bad case of the flu. Then two days later, "I got so stiff I couldn't bend my knees. A friend helped me over to the emergency room. There, I finally had a blood test, and the doctor said, 'Welcome to hepatitis B. You're very infectious.'" Diane felt miserable for a month, but then she recovered completely.[1]

Hepatitis is not always easy to diagnose. The early symptoms are very much like those of the flu, and some people have no symptoms at all—only a blood test gives the infection away. Some cases are quite obvious, though. A doctor might suspect right away that a person has hepatitis if the patient comes in with yellowish skin, or complains of dark urine. Often, a friend or relative notices a strange skin coloration and insists that the person go to the doctor.

When hepatitis is suspected, blood tests may be done to measure how well the liver is functioning. If the tests show that the liver is not functioning properly, more blood tests must be done to find out which virus is causing the hepatitis. These blood tests may test for the virus itself or for antibodies to that virus that have been built up by the body.

Diagnosing Hepatitis A

When blood tests for liver enzymes called transaminases show signs of liver damage, HAV infection can be diagnosed by testing for antibodies to the virus. The virus itself may also be detected in stool samples, using an electron microscope.

Blood Tests for Hepatitis B

Several hepatitis B tests can detect signs of HBV even before symptoms develop. Doctors usually diagnose hepatitis B by testing the blood for a protein, hepatitis B surface antigen (HBsAg), that is found on the surface of the virus. Most people who develop acute hepatitis B have HBsAg in their blood even before symptoms develop. The surface antigen disappears when a person recovers, meaning that the body has gotten rid of the virus. If, after 6 months, HBsAg is still present, it could be a sign that the person has become a

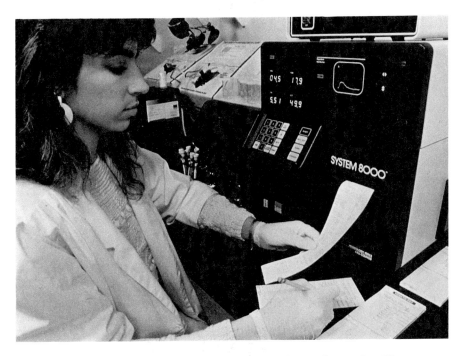

Blood tests are necessary to measure how well the liver is functioning. Here, a medical technician is performing blood tests with a blood analysis machine.

chronic carrier. Antibodies to the surface antigen (anti-HBs) remain in the body for many years to protect a person from future HBV infections.

Another identifying antigen is the hepatitis B core antigen (HBcAg) found inside the virus. There are no commercial tests available to detect HBcAg, because a complicated procedure is needed to strip away the outer coat of the virus. However, antibodies to the core antigen (anti-HBc) can usually be detected during acute hepatitis B. Over a period of time, the levels of anti-HBc decrease for most people. Those who become chronic carriers, however, usually have high levels of anti-HBc, perhaps for the rest of their lives.

Hepatitis e antigen (HBeAg) is another protein found in the virus core. Laboratory tests can detect the e antigen, as well as antibodies against it (anti-HBe). When e antigen is detected, it is an indication that the person is highly contagious. Detection of anti-HBe is often a sign that the person is less contagious.

Hepatitis C—Harder to Diagnose

Tests for other hepatitis viruses are not as revealing as those for hepatitis A and B. In 1990 doctors began using a test that could identify the antibodies against hepatitis C that are present in more than 50 percent of those with acute hepatitis C and almost all those with chronic hepatitis C. Even more sensitive tests are being developed to detect infected patients earlier, but they still cannot tell how severe the condition is and whether or not the person will become a chronic carrier.

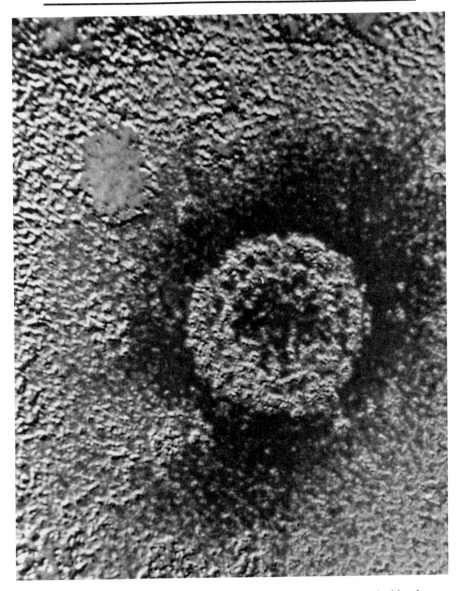

In order to diagnose hepatitis B in a patient, doctors usually test the blood for hepatitis B surface antigen (HBsAg). It is a protein which is found on the surface of the virus. Above is the hepatitis B virus, greatly magnified.

Before 1990 doctors could diagnose hepatitis C only by ruling out other possibilities. (That situation was reflected in the old name for this form, "non-A, non-B hepatitis.") But doctors still cannot detect *all* cases of hepatitis C with blood tests, at least right away. Hepatitis C antibodies may not develop for two to six months after infection, so only two-thirds of patients who go to the doctor with possible hepatitis C infection can be diagnosed with blood tests. Diagnosis may have to exclude other possible causes such as HAV, HBV, cytomegalovirus, or Epstein-Barr virus infection, as well as nonviral liver problems such as alcohol- or drug-related diseases. The patient may need to be retested for HCV for up to a year if the cause has not been found.[2]

Other Diagnostic Hepatitis Tests

In the past, delta hepatitis could be diagnosed only by a liver biopsy—surgically removing and then examining a small piece of liver tissue. However, researchers have developed a test to detect the virus's genetic material in the patient's blood. Another test can determine whether or not antibodies against a certain protein inside the hepatitis D virus are present.

Hepatitis E virus can be detected in stool samples, but there is not yet a blood test to diagnose hepatitis E.

Testing in Pregnant Women

Testing is especially important for pregnant women. Every pregnant woman should be tested for hepatitis B early in the pregnancy because the virus can be transmitted to her baby.

Up to 90 percent of babies born to infected women may develop lifelong hepatitis, and many develop complications such as cirrhosis of the liver and liver cancer many years later.

If a mother tests positive for hepatitis B, the baby is vaccinated when it is born and then twice more during the first year, to reduce the possibility of later complications.

Follow-up Tests

Follow-up blood tests are very important for hepatitis B and C patients—to find out whether they have become hepatitis virus carriers. Therefore, the blood tests for antibodies are usually repeated three and six months after the original illness. From 5 to 10 percent of hepatitis B patients and most hepatitis C sufferers become carriers.[3]

Blood-Donor Testing

Many people have no idea that they are hepatitis carriers. They have no symptoms and feel fine, but they are at higher risk for developing severe liver problems, and they can spread the disease. Some people discover they have hepatitis when they go to donate blood and are informed that their blood is unacceptable because they are infected with hepatitis.

Testing donor blood is an important step in preventing the spread of hepatitis. About 3.5 million people receive transfusions each year. Effective hepatitis B tests have greatly reduced the chances of a patient developing this disease after a transfusion. But until a reliable hepatitis C test was introduced in 1990, hepatitis C was still an important risk factor. The problem with hepatitis C is that some people do not develop antibodies until a number of months after infection, but meanwhile they are still contagious. In March 1992, an even more sensitive test for hepatitis C antibodies and enzymes that indicate liver inflammation was introduced to help eliminate more of the potentially infective blood.

6

Treating Hepatitis

n 1985, twenty-six-year-old Debbie Gregoire of Phoenix, Arizona, came down with hepatitis C after a blood transfusion she received during the birth of her first child. She developed jaundice and a rash on her leg, but both went away after a few months. A year later, she was feeling extremely tired all the time, and she went to the doctor. Tests revealed that she was still infected with the virus. Her doctor recommended she enroll in a federally sponsored experimental study using alpha interferon, a genetically engineered version of a natural immune-boosting protein in the body. After six months, the virus went into remission. Unfortunately, researchers have found that the virus often becomes active again after treatment is stopped. However, three years later, Debbie was still feeling better.[1]

A Lack of Treatments for Hepatitis

Doctors do not have many choices for treating most viral illnesses. A virus takes over body cells, forcing them to help it reproduce. Most antiviral drugs kill the infected cells as well as the virus—and the treatment can sometimes cause more problems than the virus itself. In hepatitis, like most viral diseases, the standard approach is still centered on treating symptoms and generally strengthening the body.

For all types of hepatitis, patients have traditionally been urged to get plenty of rest so that the body can fight the virus on its own. Eating a well-balanced diet is encouraged. And the patient is told to avoid alcohol and any other drugs that can put strain on the liver.

People who think they have hepatitis should see a doctor right away. They may have to go to a liver specialist (a hepatologist) or a gastroenterologist if they have a severe case or if complications arise.

Boosting the Immune System

Doctors have had some success in treating hepatitis with substances that boost the immune system. Researchers at the University of Florida in Gainesville and the NIH reported in 1989 that alpha interferon helped prevent chronic hepatitis C from getting worse in some patients. Researchers at Washington University in St. Louis, Missouri, reported similar results in chronic hepatitis B sufferers. In 1992 alpha interferon, marketed as Intron A, was approved by the FDA for these types of hepatitis.

Alpha interferon seems to work better the sooner it is used after infection. Studies have found that up to 50 percent of chronic hepatitis C sufferers and 30 to 40 percent of chronic hepatitis B sufferers show marked improvement.[2] However, in many cases of hepatitis C the symptoms get worse again when the treatment is stopped. (In one study, half of the chronic hepatitis C sufferers who had responded to alpha interferon had a relapse within six months after treatment stopped.[3] Thus only 25 percent of HCV patients respond favorably without relapsing.)

The six months of injections three times a week are expensive ($75 a week). Many patients also suffer side effects, such as flulike symptoms, a reduction in the number of disease-fighting white blood cells, and a decreased number of platelets in the blood. (Platelets are needed for blood clotting, which prevents us from bleeding to death from a cut.)

Interferon has helped some with chronic delta hepatitis also, but not as much as it has those with hepatitis B and C. Other studies, however, have reported no improvement in hepatitis D patients.

Liver Transplants

At age fifty, *Newsweek* bureau chief Frank Maier felt exhausted and began to have sudden nosebleeds and dizzy spells. Tests showed that he had "smoldering hepatitis," caused by HCV. The virus had multiplied silently over a period of years, without any symptoms, and had caused serious liver damage. The impaired liver circulation had also led to the formation of "varices" (flabby, varicose veins) in Frank's esophagus. He was warned that the varices might break open at any time, and he could bleed to death. Over the next few years there were several frantic trips to the emergency room to treat sudden hemorrhages. Meanwhile, the poisons that the damaged liver could no longer filter out of his blood were beginning to affect Frank's brain. He found it increasingly difficult to write, and he could not read the books friends sent him. He tried to "keep a feel for words" by writing in a diary, but it was often a frustrating experience. "I feel like a leaf falling too soon in the early autumn, at a time when the other leaves are still green," he laboriously printed one night.[4] He was already prepared to die when doctors recommended a liver transplant. The operation was a success. Though he must take immune-suppressing drugs to prevent his body from rejecting the new liver, "I've lived to see my second son, Danny, marry and my first grandchild, Matthew, christened," he writes. "I hope to take him to his first Cubs' game, as my grandfather did with me."[5]

Fortunately, most people with hepatitis do not suffer such severe liver damage. And, in fact, the liver can continue to function until nearly two-thirds of it is damaged. But when this happens drastic measures must be taken or the patient will die. Some chronic hepatitis sufferers may be given a liver transplant. Patients with hepatitis C acquired from blood transfusions have shown good results after liver transplants. Those with active hepatitis B, however, may not be given a transplant because the chances of reinfection of the new transplanted liver are high.[6]

Other Treatments

Doctors are exploring the use of other medications to fight hepatitis. The antiviral drugs vidarabine and acyclovir are experimental treatments for chronic hepatitis B.[7] Acyclovir was not effective for hepatitis C infection, though, and neither were corticosteroids.[8] A natural hormonelike substance, prostaglandin E, may help those with fulminant hepatitis.[9]

By 1993 Naomi Judd's symptoms had improved after she completed a course of alpha-interferon therapy. But she and many other sufferers hope that the work scientists are doing now will help bring more effective treatments and may one day wipe out hepatitis.[10]

7

Preventing Hepatitis

Lilly, an operating room nurse in an inner-city hospital in Detroit, was accidentally pricked by a needle while in the operating room, but she didn't think anything of it. Much later, when she was pregnant with her first baby, a hepatitis test revealed that she had been infected with hepatitis. And she was now an infectious carrier, even though she had no symptoms.

The doctor said there wasn't any cure, and that she might develop liver problems later on. But what really worried Lilly was that she could transmit the disease to her husband and new baby. "I was devastated, but the doctor calmed me down. He quietly and deliberately spelled out exactly what I had to do to protect my family."[1] Her husband, Nick, tested negative for hepatitis B and was vaccinated. Their baby girl was given immune globulin and vaccinated when she was born, and then vaccinated again one month later and five months after that. Neither Nick nor the baby developed hepatitis.

For hepatitis, "prevention is the best and most effective treatment," says Dr. Ira S. Goldman at North Shore University Hospital–Cornell University Medical College in Manhasset, New York.[2] One of the most effective ways of preventing any viral disease is the use of vaccines that provide protection against infection. The development of a hepatitis B vaccine is one of medicine's success stories.

Developing a Hepatitis B Vaccine

Scientists were surprised when they saw how many virus particles were present in hepatitis B–infected blood. But they were even more surprised by the smaller, nonreproducing particles. There were as many as a billion to a trillion particles in a milliliter of blood. Why would the virus cause the production of so many particles that cannot reproduce? One theory is that the smaller particles act as decoys for antibodies. If the antibodies attach to the decoys, they can't attack the viruses.

Researchers thought they might be able to use the virus particles to fight the virus. Maurice Hilleman of Merck Sharp & Dohme Research Laboratories was one of the researchers interested in hepatitis. He thought "maybe there's enough antigen in blood plasma to make a vaccine."[3] He began to try to figure out how to get large quantities of purified antigens. Dr. Baruch Blumberg was also thinking up theoretical ways of using the antigen to produce a vaccine.

Meanwhile, the pioneering hepatitis researcher, Saul Krugman, was conducting his own experiments. He took serum containing the hepatitis B virus and boiled it for one minute. Then, when he injected it into children at Willowbrook State School, he found that not only didn't they come down with hepatitis, they were also immune to it. Boiling the virus for one minute had destroyed its ability to cause disease, but had left the surface antigens able to stimulate the body to produce antibodies.

"I don't like to call it a vaccine, because it really wasn't a vaccine," Krugman says. "It demonstrated that a plasma-derived vaccine might indeed be developed. What was needed then was for the vaccine manufacturers with their highly sophisticated technology to follow up our lead."[4]

His discovery spurred on others, such as Maurice Hilleman, to come up with a vaccine. Hilleman has helped develop more human vaccines than any other person; these include vaccines against measles, mumps, rubella, chicken pox, influenza, and meningitis. But the one for hepatitis B was the most difficult.

Usually vaccines are made by growing the viruses in the laboratory and then modifying them to make them unable to reproduce. But the hepatitis B virus wouldn't grow in the lab. Krugman had shown that a vaccine could be made from the blood of people who suffered from hepatitis. But the problem was to make the vaccine safe. Scientists had to be sure the vaccine wasn't contaminated with "live" hepatitis viruses—or

Maurice Hilleman developed more human vaccines than any other person, but creating a vaccine for hepatitis B was his biggest challenge.

any other viruses, for that matter. (Remember the yellow fever vaccine contaminated with hepatitis viruses that caused widespread illness during World War II.)

Hilleman began a purification process that was aimed at making the vaccine "deader than dead."[5] Technicians wore sterile gowns, masks, and gloves, and did much of the purification by remote control. This was necessary because the plasma was highly infectious—a twentieth of a billionth part of one liter could infect a roomful of people.

The red blood cells were separated out of hepatitis-infected blood by spinning them in a centrifuge. Then the surface particles were separated from the virus by centrifuging them at a higher speed. The larger virus and much of the proteins in the blood settled to the bottom; the lighter, smaller particles stayed on top. Digestive enzymes were used to destroy impurities. The particles were then treated with urea and formaldehyde. In 1974—$70 million later—Hilleman had finished the vaccine. Tests in chimpanzees showed it was very effective and safe.

The first human trials were conducted on executives at Merck, where the vaccine was being developed. (Saul Krugman and his wife were also in the first group of human volunteers.) After six months it was confirmed that the vaccine was safe for humans. Now trials had to be begun to see whether it was effective in preventing hepatitis. Hundreds of health-professional volunteers were vaccinated, and they produced antibodies. The researchers were also able to work out the best dosages for the vaccine.

Next a large population had to be tested. This was done by a team of researchers headed by Wolf Szmuness at the New York Blood Center. The researchers decided to test it on the gay male community because, although the general incidence of hepatitis B in the United States is 5 percent, among sexually active homosexual men more than 50 percent were either currently or previously infected. A massive campaign to find volunteers was begun in the spring of 1978. By January 1979 trials began on over one thousand HBV-negative volunteers. More than 90 percent of the volunteers finished the study—receiving all three vaccinations and numerous follow-up tests. In the study only 3 percent of those vaccinated developed hepatitis B; 27 percent of the group that

WHO SHOULD BE VACCINATED?[6]

- All babies, beginning at birth
- Adolescents who are sexually active or inject drugs
- Others who engage in high-risk behaviors, including sex with multiple partners or IV drug use
- People living with a hepatitis patient or carrier
- People with hemophilia
- People whose jobs expose them to human blood

received a placebo (an injection that did not contain any active ingredients) developed the disease, mainly through sexual activity with infected partners.

The results of the study were published in October 1980. In November 1981 the U.S. Food and Drug Administration approved the vaccine—twenty-five years after Krugman began his experiments at Willowbrook and ten years after he had come up with his "homemade vaccine."

Using the Vaccine

Infants, children, and adults can all be vaccinated. The vaccine is given in three doses over a period of six months. "The hepatitis B vaccine can protect babies and children for more than ten years, and side effects are negligible," says Saul Krugman.[7] Healthy people who are vaccinated are 90 to 95 percent protected for at least seven years. A booster shot may be necessary to prolong immunity.

Protecting Health-Care Workers

Pam, a dental hygienist, was accidentally stuck with a needle used to inject novocaine in a patient. The patient was one of the many unknowing chronic carriers. Pam developed a bad case of hepatitis and was in bed for two months. She recovered, but now she makes sure she always wears gloves and a mask while treating patients. Health experts advise these practices for all health-care workers.[8]

Health experts are trying to find ways of reducing the number of hepatitis cases contracted by health-care workers.

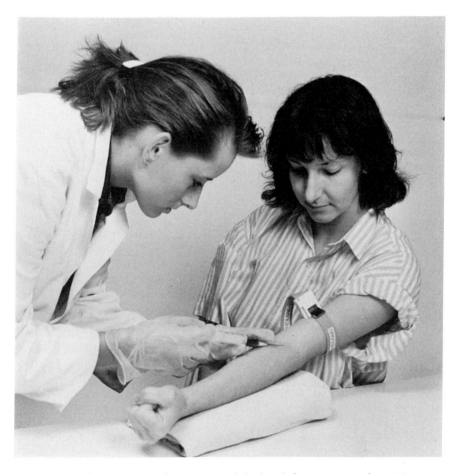

Because health-care workers are at such high risk for contracting hepatitis, they use many precautions, including the wearing of rubber gloves, when working with patients or body fluids.

Needlesticks are the most common way blood-carried diseases are spread among this group. It is estimated that needles accidentally stick health-care workers 800,000 times a year.[9] Precautions, such as wearing gloves, prevent only one out of three needlestick injuries. More than fifty products, including IV connectors, needle guards, sheathed syringes, needle-recapping products, blood-drawing devices, IV catheters, and needleless injection devices have been approved by the FDA to prevent needlestick injuries. In pilot studies conducted at ten New York hospitals, needlestick injuries were reduced 75 to 94 percent when these devices were used.[10]

Cheaper, "Safer" Vaccines

Today, most hepatitis B vaccine is made using genetic engineering. The hepatitis B vaccine was the world's first genetically-engineered vaccine. The vaccine is prepared in yeast. The gene that makes the hepatitis B surface antigen is inserted into the chromosomes of yeast cells. The yeast cells manufacture the antigen in addition to their own cell products. By using a genetically engineered vaccine, "you get rid of that nagging doubt in people's minds: 'It's a blood product— am I going to get AIDS? Am I going to get other diseases?' This new vaccine will be cheaper as well," says Dr. Hilleman.[11] The price of the hepatitis B vaccine has come down, but it is still expensive. By the early 1990s the cost was between $7 and $10 a dose for infants but four times that amount for adults. Around the world other manufacturers are producing

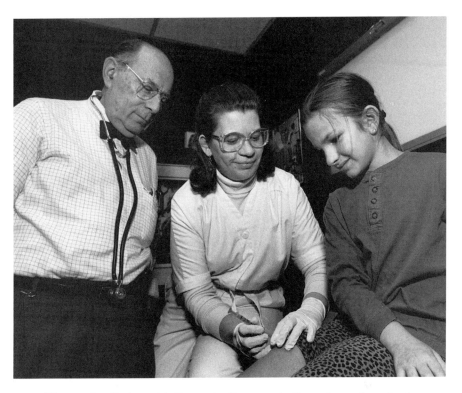

The vaccine for hepatitis B was the first genetically engineered vaccine in the world. Here, a doctor and nurse in New Jersey give a nine-year-old girl a vaccination for hepatitis B.

cheaper vaccines. A Korean company, for example, offers the vaccine at less than a dollar a dose.

Widespread Vaccinations Are Needed

"The hepatitis B story is a success story. If you could make the vaccine available to the world, then you'd *really* have a success story," says Dr. Harvey Alter.[12] "With increased awareness, hepatitis B could be totally preventable one day. If widespread vaccination programs can be implemented—such as the ones that eliminated polio—this disease can be eliminated too," says Dr. David A. Shafritz, director of the Liver Research Center at the Albert Einstein College of Medicine in New York City.[13]

Tackling Hepatitis A

In recent years, Oregon, California, Washington, and other states have had outbreaks of hepatitis A. In the early 1980s there were between 300 and 700 cases of hepatitis a year in Washington State; by 1987 there were 2500.[14] In Tacoma, Washington, the problem got so bad that health officials distributed bumper stickers reading "Dirty Hands Spread Disease: Wash Them" to try to fight the epidemic.

Hepatitis A Vaccine

Until the 1990s, immune globulin (a blood substance containing ready-made antibodies from a person who had recovered from the disease) was all doctors could use to help prevent hepatitis A outbreaks. It wasn't easy to make a vaccine for hepatitis A because the A virus mutates more often than the hepatitis B virus. But during 1992, two hepatitis A vaccines were announced. Alan Werszberger of the Kiryas Joel Institute of Medicine in Monroe, New York, led a research team that announced the successful test of an experimental vaccine in August 1992. In Europe a different hepatitis vaccine went on the market that same year.

Some experts recommend the hepatitis A vaccine be given to all children in day care, and also to travelers and others at risk for infection. But Dr. Werzberger points out that, although we now have a hepatitis A vaccine, "there can be no impact until it is universally used." Dr. William Bancroft of

IF A FAMILY MEMBER HAS HEPATITIS A . . .

If family members have hepatitis A, they should use their own towels—and, ideally, use their own bathroom when possible. They must wash their hands thoroughly after going to the bathroom. They should never share toothbrushes or razors—these items could carry contaminated blood. Some experts also suggest that they eat with disposable utensils, plates, and cups.[15]

Family members don't have to worry about catching the disease by being in the same room or touching the hepatitis patient. But it is a good idea to take precautions like wearing rubber gloves when cleaning up body fluids or feces.

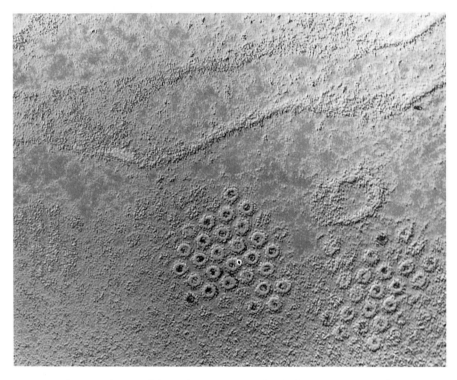

Until 1992, doctors did not have a vaccine for the hepatitis A virus, shown here greatly magnified.

the U.S. Army Medical Research and Development Council in Frederick, Maryland, agrees and has stated that vaccination "may prove to be the most cost-effective method of protecting large populations both nationally and universally."[16]

A vaccine is not yet available for hepatitis C. Vaccination for hepatitis D is not necessary—preventing hepatitis B prevents hepatitis D, too.

Other Preventive Measures

The CDC reports that alcoholic drinks such as wine or whiskey may protect against hepatitis A infection. In Florida there was an outbreak of hepatitis A after a group of people ate oysters. Those who drank alcohol while they ate the oysters were less likely to develop the disease. The researchers of the CDC study believe that alcohol may block or somehow reduce transmission of the virus into the circulatory system.[17]

Fifty-eight people in Tennessee developed hepatitis A. The outbreak was traced to a cook at a restaurant where nearly all of the people had eaten. A worker from a factory picked up hamburgers there for himself and twelve co-workers. He ate his hamburger on the drive back, but the other twelve microwaved theirs for thirty seconds. He was the only one in the factory group who developed hepatitis. Investigators studying this outbreak concluded that microwaving contaminated food seems to protect against hepatitis infection.[18]

Heating water contaminated by hepatitis E virus at 40 to 50°C (about 105 to 120°F) is enough to destroy that virus.

PREVENTING HEPATITIS

Hepatitis A and E

Good sanitation practices keep these two pretty much under control. Neither is much of a problem in the United States except in high-risk groups. Proper hand washing will keep the disease from spreading in a family.

Hepatitis B, C, and D

Preventive measures are the same as for AIDS:

- IV drug users should not share needles. (Even better would be to enter a drug treatment program or take other measures to kick the habit.)
- To avoid sexual transmission, health experts advise practicing abstinence or establishing a monogamous relationship with a person who isn't infected; practice "safer sex" and use condoms; get a hepatitis B vaccination.

Current blood tests for screening blood supplies are more accurate than ever before, but as much as one percent of all blood supplies may still cause hepatitis. So it's best for people planning to have surgery to arrange for their own blood to be used if transfusions are needed.

Preventing Liver Cancer

Since hepatitis B is one of the major causes of liver cancer, the vaccine against it is, in a way, the world's first cancer vaccine. Eliminating HBV by vaccinating children would eliminate delta as well, since it can't reproduce without HBV. Thus, it would eliminate what Georgetown University researcher John Gerin calls "one of the ten most prevalent cancers in the world and one of the most frequent cancers in developing countries."[19] Now that doctors know that other cancers may be caused by viruses, the hope is that vaccines will be developed to help fight other cancers, too.

After Exposure to a Person with Hepatitis

Those in close contact with a hepatitis A patient (such as someone who has shared a table, toilet, or bed) should receive immune globulin within two weeks of exposure.

"People who suspect that they have been exposed to hepatitis B should immediately get a shot of hepatitis B immune globulin [HBIG], a protein substance that stimulates the immune system to prevent disease. Then they should be vaccinated," says Dr. Ira S. Goldman.[20] If hepatitis B vaccine is given with HBIG within seven days of exposure, it is 90 percent effective in preventing the disease from developing.

8
Hepatitis and Society

Lou, a dentist, spent three months in the hospital and nearly a year more at home recovering from a severe case of hepatitis B. He had caught it on the job, from a patient who was a chronic hepatitis carrier. Tom, a police officer, came down with severe hepatitis B after being infected on a routine drug bust. He was stuck by a hypodermic needle while searching through a drawer for evidence. Lee, a graduate student, received a medical injection from a local doctor while vacationing in Pakistan. A month later she was in the hospital with fulminant liver failure. Barbara, a widow, took a Caribbean cruise and had a brief romantic affair with the ship's social director. Several months later, though, her pleasant memories turned sour when she developed severe hepatitis B.[1] Karen, a high school senior, used a fake ID to get a tattoo without asking her parents' permission. Two months later she had to tell her parents after all, when she got sick and tested positive for hepatitis B. Now she's a chronic carrier.[2]

These incidents sound very much like the kind of nightmare scenarios that ignited widespread hysteria in the mid-1980s as awareness of the AIDS problem spread. In various communities during that period, ambulance workers refused to transport AIDS patients to the hospital, funeral parlor employees refused to handle the bodies of people who had died of AIDS, and firefighters and rescue squad workers began to use special plastic shields when giving mouth-to-mouth resuscitation. Ironically, there has been none of that hysteria in the public reaction to the spread of hepatitis, even though HBV, for example, is more common and far more contagious than the virus that causes AIDS, and it is transmitted in much the same ways.

In fact, efforts to control and prevent hepatitis have been hampered by widespread public indifference. Eileen Johnson, who was in a coma for ten days with acute hepatitis and was not strong enough to return to work until two years later, is especially bothered by the casual way her friends and co-workers regard hepatitis. "They just don't realize how easily they can become infected with hepatitis," she says. "A lot of them say to me, 'You stay in bed a couple of weeks—what's the big deal?'"[3]

And yet, hepatitis costs society a lot in terms of lives, suffering, and money. In 1982 the CDC estimated that hepatitis B infections cost the economy $1 million a day in hospital and drug costs and lost days, weeks, or months of work. Today, with many more cases, the costs are far higher.[4] Ironically, many hepatitis cases—and much of the suffering—could be prevented.

Why No Reduction in Hepatitis?

The vaccine for hepatitis B has proved to be safe and effective, but not much progress has been made in ridding the world of hepatitis. In fact, the number of infected people has increased.

Why? One reason is that the vaccine, which works by stimulating the body to produce antibodies, isn't effective in those whose immune systems aren't functioning properly. So these people, such as dialysis patients, are at high risk for contracting the disease and yet are not protected properly. Moreover, the people at highest risk, such as intravenous drug users, are the hardest to reach. The incidence in the gay community, on the other hand, has decreased—not so much because of the hepatitis vaccine, but because of a change to safer sex practices due to a fear of AIDS. So far such changes in behavior have not become widespread among sexually active heterosexuals, most of whom do not seriously consider themselves at risk for AIDS, much less hepatitis. About 75 percent of hepatitis B cases in the United States occur in people between the ages of 18 and 39—sexually active adults. But only one percent of Americans in this age group have been vaccinated.[5]

Health-care workers who handle blood are required to be vaccinated. But many health-care workers who might accidentally come in contact with infected blood or other body fluids have not yet received the vaccine—by the early 1990s only 50 percent of health-care workers had been vaccinated against hepatitis B. Even this number took a long time, since a vaccine has been available since 1981. Many health-care workers had been reluctant because they didn't think they were at risk for contracting the disease, or they were hesitant about receiving a vaccine made from a blood product because of the fear of AIDS. By the early 1990s 12,000 health-care workers were still being infected each year. About 250 were still dying yearly from complications of HBV after being infected on the job.[6]

Another reason hepatitis hasn't been conquered is that, as

AIDS PARALLELS

The AIDS epidemic emerged into public awareness shortly after tests of the hepatitis B vaccine among the gay community of New York concluded. The researchers realized that the blood samples and questionnaires that had been gathered could also provide invaluable information about how many people had AIDS, how fast the infection was spreading, and the rate at which people become ill and die from AIDS. Each year the findings are updated. Many of the original men in the study are continuing with periodic blood testing and examinations to shed new light on AIDS.[7]

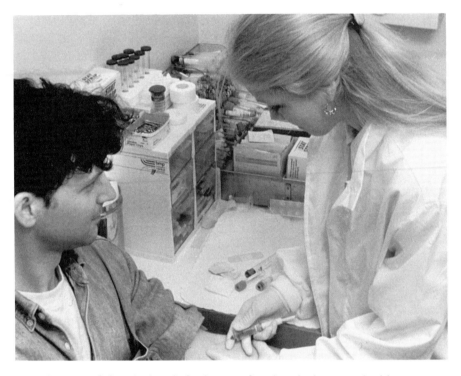

Because of their high risk for being infected with the virus, health-care workers are required to be vaccinated for hepatitis B.

Dr. Robert Purcell, head of the Hepatitis Viruses Section at the NIH, points out, "forty percent of hepatitis B cases in the U.S. are associated with no known exposure to the virus. That means that we probably still don't understand how the virus is spread in the general population. So unless you immunize the whole population, you're just not going to have a very great impact." Worldwide, "the problem is that the people who need it the most, Asians and Africans, can't afford it," says NIH researcher Dr. Harvey Alter.[8]

Immunizing Children

To wipe out hepatitis B, society can't just concentrate on high-risk groups. Dr. Martha Lepow at Albany Medical College in New York says, "The cases recognized each year have been going up. You can't predict who is high-risk now. All children today are potentially at risk."[9]

Health officials have been unsuccessful in their efforts to get high-risk groups vaccinated, so in 1991 the CDC recommended that all infants be given three hepatitis B vaccine doses before the age of eighteen months. Infants already receive other vaccinations, so they are an easier group to reach. The first dose should be given while the baby is in the hospital, the second dose at one to two months of age, and the third at six to eighteen months. Babies born to infected mothers should receive the vaccine plus hepatitis B antibodies as soon as possible after birth, with additional doses at one month and at six months. The American Academy of Pediatrics endorsed the practice in February 1992. The CDC estimates that by following these guidelines, 90 percent of chronic hepatitis B in the United States will be eliminated by the year 2015. In Hawaii, where the program has been in effect, the acute hepatitis B rate has dropped from 200 cases per 100,000 population in 1982 down to less than 10 per 100,000 in the early 1990s.[10]

The Vaccination Controversy

Doctors and patients have resisted the hepatitis vaccination program. They complain about the high price of the vaccinations, and many are skeptical about potential benefits. "Parents say, 'My kid isn't going to be a drug abuser or a

ADOLESCENTS ARE AT RISK

The American Academy of Pediatrics advises immunizing children and adolescents because hepatitis B occurs mostly in adolescents and young adults in the United States. But in the years after a vaccination, the antibody levels may gradually decline. So adolescents who were vaccinated as babies may have low levels of antibodies and thus may not be fully protected from the disease. If they are sexually active, they may increase their risk of developing hepatitis B. For these reasons some doctors are now recommending that a booster shot be given to young people at puberty. Some recommend giving a booster every five years.[11]

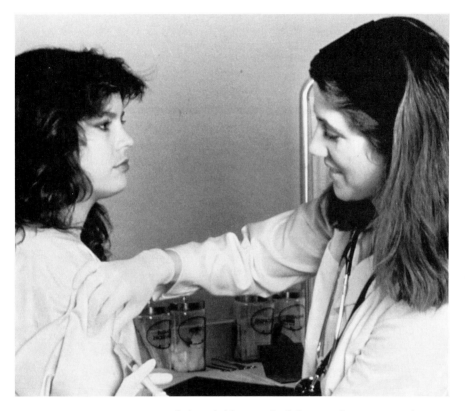

Doctors now recommend that children and adolescents be immunized, and given a booster shot when they are older to ensure the vaccine is still effective.

homosexual,'" says Dr. Edgar Marcuse at the University of Washington in Seattle, who helped formulate the American Academy of Pediatrics' recommendations. "You then say, 'How can you predict if your kid may one day be the sexual partner of someone at high risk?' Most parents will accept that."[12] In addition, although hepatitis B is most common in adolescents and young adults in the United States, everyone living in the same household as an infected person is also at risk, because the hepatitis B virus is more easily spread than the virus that causes AIDS. Cuts, scrapes, or other breaks in the skin could allow infected blood or other body fluids into the body.

Many doctors feel hesitant, too. There is still uncertainty about how long the vaccine is good for. An adolescent or young adult may be at high risk just when the vaccine is starting to lose effectiveness. Proponents say it works for at least a decade and a single booster shot may be all that is necessary to give further immunity. Moreover, children under five who are infected are the most likely to become carriers, so by immunizing all children, the infection is at worst delayed until a later time when the likelihood of becoming a carrier is lowered. (Vaccinating babies born to infected mothers reduces the risk of their becoming chronic carriers from 90% down to 5%.)

"Universal immunization of our children is the only way to ensure protection from hepatitis B and the illness and death it causes," says Dr. Richard Duma, executive director of the National Foundation for Infectious Diseases in Bethesda, Maryland.[13]

9
Hepatitis and the Future

Scientists have made a lot of progress toward getting hepatitis under control. Work is underway in many different areas to bring about better ways to prevent, treat, and cure the various forms of hepatitis. Genetic engineering has helped researchers tremendously in understanding the basic biology of HBV and the way it causes infection and cancer. Genetic technology has produced more sensitive diagnostic tests and is providing better vaccines, not only against HBV but against other hepatitis viruses as well. Genetically engineered interferon helps some patients, too.

Scientists are also learning a great deal about hepatitis through animal research. The woodchuck is being used to test vaccines and drugs for HBV, HCV, and HDV, for example, because it develops a disease similar to acute and chronic hepatitis in humans.[1] Transgenic mice—mice that have viral genes inserted into their own genes—are also helping to provide a better understanding of hepatitis infections in humans.

Why Men Have More Problems With HBV

Christine Pourcel of the Pasteur Institute used transgenic mice to discover why HBV prefers liver cells. She found that one of the HBV genes is present in high levels only in liver tissue, where it is controlled by steroid hormones. Men have higher natural steroid levels than women, which helps explain why men are at greater risk for chronic HBV infection, liver damage, and liver cancer.[2]

Role of the Hepatitis Virus in Cancer

More than 80 percent of liver cancers worldwide have been linked to hepatitis B, but it is not certain how HBV causes cancer. The virus might directly trigger the development of tumors, or the tumor might develop after chronic inflammation and cirrhosis. (There are more chances for cancer-causing mutations to occur when diseased tissue regenerates.)

Some researchers believe that liver cancer is caused directly by the virus, and is not an indirect result after HBV first causes hepatitis. Experiments with transgenic mice have found that a protein made by one of the virus's genes may be responsible for causing liver cancer. Gilbert Jay at the Jerome N. Holland Laboratory of the American Red Cross in Rockville, Maryland, and colleagues at Japan's National Institute of Health discovered a protein called the HBx antigen. This antigen is produced by a hepatitis gene. The researchers inserted the HBx gene into mouse embryos so that the virus gene would be a part of the mouse genes. The HBx antigen was present in their livers, kidneys, and testes. By ten months, the transgenic mice were beginning to develop liver tumors, and by fifteen months most had died of these tumors. None of the normal mice developed liver tumors. "Our findings provide overwhelming evidence for the direct involvement of HBV in the development of liver cancer," the researchers say.[3]

Dr. John Taylor of the Fox Chase Cancer Center in Philadelphia points out that another gene from the virus has also been shown to cause cancer in other experiments with mice.[4]

Researchers are excited at the idea that it might be possible to find new drugs to prevent liver cancer by testing them on transgenic mice that bear the cancer-causing gene. Other researchers point out, however, that it is not yet certain that the gene has the same effect in humans. Dr. William Mason at the Fox Chase Cancer Center says it is "probably one of the many factors that are going on" that might lead to liver cancer.[5]

Using One Microbe to Fight Another

When the hepatitis D virus infects a cell previously infected by hepatitis B, it "shuts down HBV." Georgetown University researcher Dr. John Gerin wonders whether a specially weakened delta virus could be used as a "stop signal" for HBV. As

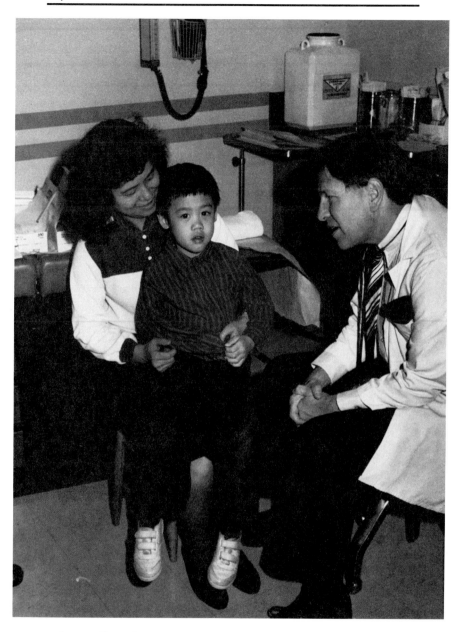

A doctor talks with a young patient at the Liver Cancer Prevention Center of the Fox Chase Cancer Center.

researchers get a better understanding of delta, they hope that they may be able to build a delta virus that "could shut off B and not cause disease."[6]

At Washington University in St. Louis, researcher Dr. Roy Curtiss is genetically engineering vaccines by combining portions of DNA from hepatitis B virus with salmonella, the bacterium that causes food poisoning and diarrhea. (The bacteria used for the vaccines are specially modified to remove the disease-causing parts.) The genetically engineered bacterial cells produce HBV antigens that stimulate immunity. Dr. Curtiss points out that salmonella vaccines would be especially valuable in developing countries because they do

---

HELP FROM AIDS RESEARCH

HBV reproduces in much the same way as the AIDS virus. Hiroki Mitsuya of the National Institutes of Health is testing drugs similar to AZT (a drug used in treating AIDS) in Peking ducks, in an effort to interrupt one of the steps in the reproduction of the virus.[7] AIDS research is helping scientists to gain a better understanding of cancer and the immune system. In fact, some researchers believe that many chronic cases of HBV and HCV develop because hepatitis viruses, like the AIDS virus, apparently mutate frequently. The body isn't able to build up effective antibodies because the changes in the virus trick its immune defenses.[8]

---

not have to be refrigerated and are cheaper to make than the bottles that would contain them.[9]

Prevention by Delay

The chance of becoming a carrier and later developing liver cancer is greatest when HBV is contracted in infancy. Dr. Baruch Blumberg says, "When I realized that we didn't have to cure HBV but could delay it and thereby prevent liver cancer, it was a real breakthrough, an important idea."[10] He looked for a way to keep an infected liver from developing into a cancerous one. Dutch researchers discovered that patients who developed HBV infection often showed a rise in iron levels in red blood cells. Iron is needed to carry oxygen in our red blood cells. But too much iron actually hinders our immune system. And bacteria, fungi, protozoa, and tumor cells need iron to grow, too. Researchers found that patients who had higher iron levels became HBV carriers more often than normal. Dr. Blumberg hopes that finding ways to control the amount of iron that is available to infected liver cells may slow down cancer development. He calls this "prevention by delay." If this "treatment" is combined with prevention through blood screening and HBV vaccine, early infection with HBV leading to liver cancer might someday be a problem of the past.[11]

Edible Vaccines

Charles J. Arntzen and colleagues at Texas A&M Institute of Biosciences and Technology in Houston think that someday vaccines won't have to be injected—we'll be able to be inoculated against diseases such as hepatitis by eating a piece of fruit.

The researchers inserted the gene that produces the hepatitis B surface antigen into tobacco plants. As new tobacco plant cells grew, the surface antigen was also produced. The researchers are now testing to see whether animals develop immunity to hepatitis B after eating the plants. "We view our recent experiments as a successful first step." They hope that eventually the research will result in low-cost edible vaccines. Current hepatitis B vaccine doses cost about $10. The researchers believe that the plant vaccine might ultimately bring the cost down to as little as 2 cents a dose. The banana is the researchers' first choice for the fruit to deliver the vaccine, because it is "the first solid food that kids get in many parts of the developing world," says Arntzen. Lettuce is another possibility.[12]

Liver Transplants

Liver transplants may be necessary when the liver is too damaged to function. But there are not enough donor livers available. Researchers are experimenting with implanting baboon livers into humans. In June 1992 a thirty-five-year-old man, dying of hepatitis B, was given the first baboon liver transplant. He died ten weeks later from an overdose of an anti-rejection drug, but researchers were excited. His body had not rejected the liver and it was functioning properly. A second patient, a sixty-two-year-old man also dying of hepatitis, received the second such transplant early in 1993.[13]

A Hepatitis E Vaccine

Genelabs researchers, working with scientists at the CDC, identified the hepatitis E virus in 1988. The researchers at Genelabs, again in collaboration with researchers at the CDC, have developed a prototype hepatitis E vaccine that is being tested on animals. In 1992 the company joined with SmithKline Beecham of Philadelphia to develop the vaccine.[14]

Other Avenues of Research

Scientists are also trying to figure out how to make antiviral drugs work to kill viruses but not harm human cells. Other researchers are studying the immune response that the body mounts against hepatitis to figure out why some people recover and others become carriers.

Alpha-interferon injections have been approved by the FDA as a treatment for hepatitis B, and the study of their effectiveness in hepatitis C is continuing. It has been found that one-third of hepatitis B patients and one-fourth of hepatitis C patients who receive this treatment recover—their liver enzyme levels return to normal. But scientists are still not sure whether this means the virus has been removed from the person's body. Meanwhile, other antiviral drugs such as ribavirin are being studied to fight hepatitis C.[15]

The fight against hepatitis is thus being staged on a variety of fronts—a fitting approach for this varied and challenging family of diseases.

Q & A

Q. Is hepatitis a disease?

A. Not exactly. It is a general name for a group of viral diseases and other conditions that result in inflammation of the liver.

Q. Could I catch hepatitis by eating food prepared by someone who has it?

A. Maybe, if someone with hepatitis A or E didn't wash his or her hands after going to the bathroom and then handled food; or if someone infected with hepatitis B or C virus bled on the food and you had an open cut in your mouth.

Q. Could I catch hepatitis by sharing a toothbrush used by someone who had it?

A. Maybe. Vigorous toothbrushing may make the gums bleed, and the hepatitis B virus can survive outside the body for a week or more.

Q. My boyfriend had hepatitis B a few years ago. Could I catch it from him?

A. Maybe. Some people continue to carry hepatitis viruses even after they have recovered from the illness. Although they are healthy, they can transmit the disease to others.

Q. Could someone who is HIV-positive catch hepatitis?

A. Yes. AIDS and hepatitis B, C, and D are transmitted in similar ways, including unsafe sex practices and needle-sharing by drug addicts, so the same high-risk behavior could expose a person to both AIDS and hepatitis. (People with a sexually transmitted disease (STD) are often found to be infected with other STDs, too.) Moreover, HIV (the AIDS virus) damages the immune system and thus lowers the body's defenses against other diseases. Thus an HIV-positive person could readily become infected by a hepatitis virus and develop a more serious illness than someone with a healthy immune system.

Q. How serious is hepatitis?

A. Some cases are so mild that the person may not notice any symptoms or may think it is the flu. Or symptoms may be more severe, including extreme fatigue that lasts for weeks, months, or even years. Some may develop serious liver problems years later. In rare cases liver damage develops rapidly and can lead to death.

Q. What's the difference between "acute" and "chronic" hepatitis?

A. Acute hepatitis is the illness that develops after the original infection. Usually the person recovers, but sometimes the disease becomes persistent and long-lasting (chronic). The person may eventually recover but remains a carrier of the virus. Or an active, debilitating illness may continue and progress to the point that it causes severe damage to the liver and other body organs.

Q. Why is liver damage so dangerous?

A. The liver helps to keep poisons from harming the body, produces many valuable body chemicals, and has about 500 other important functions. Fortunately, if it's given a chance, the liver can grow new tissues to replace damaged ones.

Q. They didn't have hepatitis vaccinations when I was a baby. Should I get vaccinated now?

A. It's a good idea. Adolescents and young adults are at the greatest risk for hepatitis, and even if you don't ever intend to do drugs or have multiple sex partners, you may be exposed to someone who is carrying the hepatitis virus. Vaccinations are especially important for people in the health-care professions.

Q. Is the hepatitis vaccine safe? Could I get AIDS from it?

A. Blood-product vaccines are specially treated to kill any viruses. Most of the hepatitis vaccines used today are made in yeast cells. So they can't contain any viruses that could cause blood-transmitted diseases.

Hepatitis Timeline

2000 B.C.—Early references to hepatitis epidemics.

1942— Contaminated yellow fever vaccine causes hepatitis epidemic among U.S. soldiers.

1956— Saul Krugman begins experiments on hepatitis at Willowbrook State School.

1963— Baruch Blumberg discovers Au antigen.

1965— Krugman isolates hepatitis viruses and establishes that they cause two different diseases.

1966— First diagnosis of hepatitis B with Au test.

1973— American Association of Blood Banks begins requiring testing of donor blood for Au antigen.

1974— Maurice Hilleman develops hepatitis B vaccine.

1975— Stephen Feinstone, Robert Purcell, and Albert Kapikian isolate hepatitis A virus and devise a blood test for it.

1977— Mario Rizzetto and John Gerin isolate the delta particle.

1981— FDA approves hepatitis B vaccine.

1986— Hepatitis B virus first grown in a test tube.

1987— Michael Houghton identifies hepatitis C virus.

1988— Daniel Bradley discovers hepatitis E virus.

1990— First reliable hepatitis C test for blood is introduced.

1991— CDC recommends that infants be immunized against hepatitis B.

1992— FDA approves alpha interferon for treatment of chronic hepatitis B and C; two hepatitis A vaccines are announced.

For More Information

American Liver Foundation
1425 Pompton Avenue
Cedar Grove, NJ 07009
(800) 223-0179
(*Toll-free hot line*)

Center for Liver Diseases
1500 N.W. 12th Avenue,
Suite 1101
Miami, FL 33136

Centers for Disease Control
Hepatitis Branch
Division of Viral and
Rickettsial Diseases
Atlanta, GA 30333
(404) 332-4555
(*CDC Hepatitis Hot line*)

Children's Liver Foundation
14245 Ventura Boulevard,
Suite 201
Sherman Oaks, CA 91423

International Association
for the Study of the Liver
VA Medical Center
Hepatic Hemodynamic
Lab/111J
West Haven, CT 06516

National Institute of Allergy
and Infectious Diseases
National Institutes of Health
Bethesda, MD 20892

SmithKline Beecham
Pharmaceuticals
One Franklin Plaza
P.O. Box 7929
Philadelphia, PA 19101
(800) HEP-B-873

(*For referral to a doctor
near you*)

Chapter Notes

Chapter 1

1. "Judd Discusses 'Monster,'" *The Courier News* (Bridgewater, N.J.), January 27, 1993, p. D2.

2. Thomas H. Maugh II, "The Many Faces of Hepatitis," *The World Book Health and Medical Annual,* 1993, p. 101.

3. Rob Stein, "The ABC's of Hepatitis," *American Health,* June 1993, p. 66.

4. Ibid.

5. Phyllis Bernstein, "Hepatitis B: The Sneaky Virus," *Cosmopolitan,* June 1992, p. 124.

Chapter 2

1. Peter Radetsky, *The Invisible Invaders* (Boston: Little, Brown, & Co., 1991), p. 256.

2. Ibid., p. 259.

3. Ibid., p. 264.

4. Ann Giudici Fettner, *Science of Viruses* (New York: William Morrow, 1990), p. 166.

5. Ibid.

6. Radetsky, p. 270.

7. Fettner, p. 167.

8. Ibid., p. 173.

9. Ibid., p. 174.

Chapter 3

1. Janice Hopkins Tanne, "The Other Plague," *New York,* July 11, 1988, p. 35.

2. Rob Stein, "The ABC's of Hepatitis," *American Health,* June 1993, p. 66.

3. Ibid., p. 68.

4. Peter Radetsky, *The Invisible Invaders* (Boston: Little, Brown, & Co., 1991), p. 293.

5. Tanne, p. 35.

6. Pierre Tiollais and Marie-Annick Buendia, "Hepatitis B Virus," *Scientific American,* April 1991, p. 117.

7. Ibid.

8. Gina Kolata, "Hepatitis C May Be Hidden Epidemic, Studies Show," *The New York Times,* December 31, 1992, p. A20.

9. "Hepatitis B Prevention." Pamphlet from the CDC/NCID, Division of Viral and Rickettsial Diseases, October 1992.

10. Kolata, "Hepatitis C May Be Hidden Epidemic, Studies Show," p. A20.

11. Ibid.

12. Radetsky, p. 288.

13. Tanne, p. 38.

14. Ibid., p. 37.

15. Richard Aach, Shalom Z. Hirschman, and Paul V. Holland, "The ABCs of Viral Hepatitis," *Patient Care,* August 15, 1992, p. 37.

16. Kolata, "Hepatitis C May Be Hidden Epidemic, Studies Show," p. A20.

17. Gina Kolata, "Mysterious Epidemic of Furtive Liver Virus," *The New York Times,* January 19, 1993, p. C3.

18. Leslie Laurence, "Beware the Quiet Killer," *Redbook,* October 1991, p. 32.

Chapter 4

1. Lawrence Galton, "Hepatitis Is Mysterious, Elusive and On the Increase," *New York Times Magazine,* October 13, 1968, p. 152.

2. Rob Stein, "The ABC's of Hepatitis," *American Health,* June 1993, p. 66.

3. Jonathan Turley, "We Need to Unearth Environmental Felons," *The Wall Street Journal,* March 11, 1993, p. A15.

4. Janice Hopkins Tanne, "The Other Plague," *New York,* July 11, 1988, p. 36.

5. Stein, p. 66.

6. *Medicine: The Year in Review* (St. Louis: Medical Tribune–Mosby, 1993), p. 192.

7. Thomas H. Maugh II, "The Many Faces of Hepatitis," in *The World Book Health and Medical Annual,* 1993, p. 101.

8. Tanne, p. 37.

9. Ibid.

10. *Medicine: The Year in Review,* p. 186.

11. Tanne, p. 37.

12. Leslie Laurence, "Beware the Quiet Killer," *Redbook,* October 1991, p. 28.

13. Stein, p. 67.

14. Sheryl L. Menacker, "Learning About HBV The Hard Way," *Medical Tribune,* June 11, 1992, p. 14.

15. Tanne, p. 38.

16. Ibid.

17. Phyllis Bernstein, "Hepatitis B: The Sneaky Virus," *Cosmopolitan,* June 1992, p. 124.

18. Tanne, p. 36.

19. Bernstein, p. 126.

20. Stein, p. 67.

21. Richard Aach, Shalom Z. Hirschman, and Paul V. Holland, "The ABCs of Viral Hepatitis," *Patient Care,* August 15, 1992, p. 46.

22. "Hepatitis B Prevention." Pamphlet from the CDC/NCID, Division of Viral and Rickettsial Diseases, October 1992.

23. Stein, p. 69.

24. Gina Kolata, "Mysterious Epidemic of Furtive Liver Virus," *The New York Times,* January 19, 1993, p. C3.

Chapter 5

1. Phyllis Bernstein, "Hepatitis B: the Sneaky Virus," *Cosmopolitan,* June 1992, p. 124.

2. Richard Aach, Shalom Z. Hirschman, and Paul V. Holland, "The ABCs of Viral Hepatitis," *Patient Care,* August 15, 1992, p. 46.

3. Ibid., p. 38.

Chapter 6

1. Leslie Laurence, "Beware the Quiet Killer," *Redbook*, October 1991, p. 32.

2. Alan M. Rees and Charlene Willey, eds., "Hepatitis," *Personal Health Reporter* (Detroit: Gale Research, 1993), p. 290.

3. Richard Aach, Shalom Z. Hirschman, and Paul V. Holland, "The ABCs of Viral Hepatitis," *Patient Care*, August 15, 1992, p. 49.

4. Frank Maier, "A Second Chance at Life," *Newsweek*, September 12, 1988, p. 54.

5. Ibid., p. 61.

6. Rees and Willey, p. 290.

7. Aach, Hirschman, and Holland, p. 40.

8. P. J. Dolan, et al., "Hepatitis C: Prevention and Treatment," *American Family Physician*, April, 1991, p. 1349.

9. Rees and Willey, p. 290.

10. Thomas H. Maugh II, "The Many Faces of Hepatitis," *The World Book Health and Medical Annual*, 1993, p. 109.

Chapter 7

1. Phyllis Bernstein, "Hepatitis B: The Sneaky Virus," *Cosmopolitan*, June 1992, p. 126.

2. Ibid.

3. Peter Radetsky, *The Invisible Invaders* (Boston: Little, Brown, & Co., 1991), p. 273.

4. Ibid., p. 274.

5. Ibid., p. 275.

6. "Hepatitis B Prevention." Pamphlet from the CDC/NCID, Division of Viral and Rickettsial Diseases, October 1992.

7. *Medicine: The Year in Review* (St. Louis: Medical Tribune–Mosby, 1993), p. 67.

8. Bernstein, p. 126.

9. Eleanor Mayfield, "Protecting Patients and Professionals from Blood-Borne Diseases," *FDA Consumer*, April 1993, p. 11.

10. Ibid., p. 13.

11. Radetsky, p. 287.

12. Ibid.

13. Bernstein, p. 126.

14. Associated Press, "Hygiene Effort Against Hepatitis," *The New York Times*, November 15, 1988, p. C1.

15. Leslie Laurence, "Beware the Quiet Killer," *Redbook*, October 1991, p. 32.

16. Charlene Laino, "One-Dose Vaccine Stops Childhood Hepatitis A," *Medicine: The Year in Review*, p. 62.

17. Ibid., p. 152.

18. B. Mishu et al., "Hepatitis A: Microwaving Food May Reduce Risk," *Modern Medicine*, February 1991, p. 127.

19. Ann Giudici Fettner, *Science of Viruses* (New York: William Morrow, 1990), p. 180.

20. Bernstein, p. 126.

Chapter 8

1. Janice Hopkins Tanne, "The Other Plague," *New York*, July 11, 1988, pp. 36–37.

2. "I Expected Getting a Tattoo to Hurt a Little. I Didn't Expect It to Almost Kill Me," *Sassy*, February 1993, p. 24.

3. Rob Stein, "The ABC's of Hepatitis," *American Health*, June 1993, p. 65.

4. Tanne, p. 38.

5. Sheryl L. Menacker, "Learning About HBV The Hard Way," *Medical Tribune*, June 11, 1992, p. 14.

6. Stein, p. 68.

7. Bruce Lambert, "10 Years Later, Hepatitis Study Still Yields Critical Data on AIDS," *The New York Times*, July 17, 1990, p. C3.

8. Peter Radetsky, *The Invisible Invaders* (Boston: Little, Brown, & Co., 1991), p. 286.

9. Andrea Kott, "AAP Now Advocates Vaccination of All Infants For Hepatitis B," *Medicine: The Year in Review* (St. Louis: Medical Tribune–Mosby, 1992), p. 58.

10. Thomas H. Maugh II, "The Many Faces of Hepatitis," *The World Book Health and Medical Annual,* 1993, p. 109.

11. Susan Baker, "Pushing for Teen Immunization," *Medicine: The Year in Review* (St. Louis: Medical Tribune–Mosby, 1993), p. 67.

12. Stein, p. 68.

13. Ibid.

Chapter 9

1. "Hepatitis." Pamphlet from the National Institute of Allergy and Infectious Diseases, August 1992, p. 5.

2. Pierre Tiollais and Marie-Annick Buendia, "Hepatitis B Virus," *Scientific American,* April 1991, p. 119.

3. "Hepatitis Gene Is Shown to Cause Liver Cancer," *New Scientist,* May 25, 1991, p. 23.

4. Associated Press, "Study Suggests a Liver Cancer Breakthrough," *The New York Times,* May 24, 1991, p. A16.

5. Ibid.

6. Ann Giudici Fettner, *Science of Viruses* (New York: William Morrow, 1993), p. 178.

7. Ibid., p. 177.

8. "Hepatitis Viruses Mutate Frequently," *Medical Tribune,* June 11, 1992, p. 10.

9. Associated Press, "Birth Control Vaccine Uses Altered Salmonella Bacteria," *The New York Times,* November 2, 1993, p. C9.

10. Fettner, p. 171.

11. Ibid., pp. 171–172.

12. Constance Holden, ed., "Getting Vaccinated for Breakfast?" *Science,* December 18, 1992, p. 1878; Bob Ortega, "Vaccine-Designing Scientists Go Bananas," *The Wall Street Journal,* March 9, 1994, p. B6.

13. Associated Press, "Doctors: Baboon Liver Working Fine in Man," *The Courier News* (Bridgewater, N.J.), January 12, 1993, p. A5.

14. Lawrence M. Fisher, "The Fruit of Collaboration: A New Hepatitis Vaccine," *The New York Times,* September 13, 1992, p. 8.

15. Gina Kolata, "Mysterious Epidemic of Furtive Liver Virus," *The New York Times,* January 19, 1993, p. C3.

Glossary

acute hepatitis—A hepatitis virus infection that clears up within six months.

acyclovir—An experimental antiviral drug.

AIDS—An acronym for acquired immune deficiency syndrome, a serious viral disease.

alpha interferon—A genetically engineered form of interferon that is used to treat hepatitis B and C.

antibodies—Proteins produced to bind specifically to foreign chemicals (antigens), such as surface chemicals on an invading virus.

Au antigen—A hepatitis B antigen originally found in the blood of an Australian aboriginal and used in a test for hepatitis B.

bilirubin—A reddish-brown bile pigment that is responsible for the yellowish color of the skin in jaundice.

carrier—A person infected with a disease microbe who, without showing any symptoms, can transmit the disease to others.

chronic hepatitis—Persistence of hepatitis virus infection for a long time (even for life), with or without symptoms. Illness may recur.

chronic persistent hepatitis—A form of hepatitis that clears up within a few years (but the person remains a carrier).

cirrhosis—Scarring of the liver.

cytomegalovirus—A common virus that can cause mononucleosis and liver damage.

delta particle—An incomplete hepatitis virus that can cause a severe form of hepatitis in people also infected with hepatitis B virus.

Epstein-Barr virus—A virus that causes mononucleosis and may damage the liver.

121

fulminant hepatitis—A very severe, rapidly developing form of hepatitis, which is often fatal. (Also called fast-progressing hepatitis.)

HBx antigen—An antigen of the hepatitis B virus.

hemophilia—A blood-clotting disorder. People with hemophilia regularly receive clotting factors taken from large numbers of donor blood specimens and are at higher risk of developing hepatitis B than those who receive a blood transfusion.

hepadnaviruses—A group of viruses that attack the liver (including the hepatitis viruses).

hepatic—Pertaining to the liver.

hepatitis—Inflammation of the liver.

hepatitis A and E viruses (HAV and HEV)—Liver-damaging viruses transmitted orally, usually by contaminated water or foods.

hepatitis B, C, and D viruses (HBV, HCV, and HDV or delta)—Liver-damaging viruses transmitted through blood (e.g., in transfusions or needle-sharing by addicts) or sexual activity.

hepatitis B surface antigen (HBsAg)—A viral surface protein that is the basis for a diagnostic test for HBV.

hepatitis core antigen (HBcAg)—A protein found inside the hepatitis B virus.

hepatologist—A doctor specializing in liver diseases.

immune globulin—A portion of donor blood containing antibodies.

immune system—Various body defenses against invading microbes, including white blood cells and interferon.

immunity—The ability to resist a disease through the action of disease-fighting cells adapted to attack an invading microbe or its products.

infectious hepatitis—An old name for hepatitis A.

inflammation—Swelling, pain, heat, and redness in the tissues around a site of infection.

interferon—A protein released by virus-infected cells that protects other cells from infection.

jaundice—A yellowing of the skin and the whites of the eyes due to a buildup of bile pigments in the blood and tissues.

necrosis—Massive damage and death of tissues.

needlestick—An accidental puncture of the skin of a health worker by a needle contaminated with a patient's blood or body fluids.

non-A, non-B hepatitis—An old name for hepatitis C. Epidemic non-A, non-B hepatitis is hepatitis E.

salmonella—A bacterium that causes food poisoning and diarrhea.

serum hepatitis—An old name for hepatitis B.

toxic hepatitis—Deterioration of liver cells due to chemicals.

transaminases—Liver enzymes whose presence in the blood may be a sign of hepatitis infection.

transgenic mice—Mice that have genes of viruses or other organisms inserted into their own hereditary material.

vaccination—administration (usually by injection or orally) of a preparation of microbes or their products to stimulate protective immunity against disease.

vidarabine—An experimental antiviral drug.

viral hepatitis—A group of contagious diseases affecting the liver, which can be caused by at least five different viruses (HAV, HBV, HCV, HDV, and HEV).

Further Reading

Books

Fettner, Ann Giudici, *Science of Viruses*. New York: William Morrow, 1990.

Radetsky, Peter, *The Invisible Invaders*. Boston: Little, Brown, & Co. 1991.

Articles

Aach, Richard, Shalom Z. Hirschman, and Paul V. Holland. "The ABCs of Viral Hepatitis." *Patient Care*, August 15, 1992, pp. 34–50.

Bernstein, Phyllis. "Hepatitis B: The Sneaky Virus." *Cosmopolitan*, June 1992, pp. 124–126.

Dolan, P. J., et al., "Hepatitis C: Prevention and Treatment." *American Family Physician*, April 1991, pp. 1347–1360.

Kolata, Gina. "Hepatitis C May Be Hidden Epidemic, Studies Show." *The New York Times*, December 31, 1992, p. A20.

Kolata, Gina. "Mysterious Epidemic of Furtive Liver Virus." *The New York Times*, January 19, 1993, pp. C1, C3.

Lambert, Bruce. "10 Years Later, Hepatitis Study Still Yields Critical Data on AIDS." *The New York Times*, July 17, 1990, p. C3.

Laurence, Leslie. "Beware the Quiet Killer." *Redbook*, October 1991, pp. 24, 28, 32.

Lee, William M. "Hepatitis Update: Diagnosis, Treatment, and Prevention." *Modern Medicine*, September 1990, pp. 46–64.

Maier, Frank. "A Second Chance at Life." *Newsweek*, September 12, 1988, pp. 52–61.

Mauth, Thomas H., II. "The Many Faces of Hepatitis." *The World Book Health and Medical Annual*, 1993, pp. 97–109.

Mayfield, Eleanor. "Protecting Patients and Professionals from Blood-Borne Disease." *FDA Consumer*, April 1993, pp. 9–13.

Stein, Rob. "The ABC's of Hepatitis." *American Health*, June 1993, pp. 65–69.

Tanne, Janice Hopkins. "The Other Plague." *New York*, July 11, 1988, pp. 34–40.

Tiollais, Pierre, and Marie-Annick Buendia. "Hepatitis B Virus." *Scientific American*, April 1991, pp. 116–123.

Whitlow, Joan. "Hepatitis Fight Goes On." *The Star-Ledger* (Newark, N.J.), May 5, 1991, pp. 15–16.

Pamphlets

U.S. Department of Health and Human Services, Public Health Service (Centers for Disease Control):

"Hepatitis C Prevention," April 1992.

"Hepatitis B Prevention and Pregnancy," August 1992.

"Hepatitis B Prevention," October 1992.

"Why Does My Baby Need Hepatitis B Vaccine?" (n.d.)

SmithKline Beecham Pharmaceuticals:

"Hepatitis B Virus Vaccine," October 1992.

Index

P

Peking ducks, 47
placebo, 80
platelets, 71
polio virus, 30
pregnant women, 49, 66–67
prevention, 74–89
primates, 43, 47
prostaglandin E, 73
Purcell, Robert, 24, 25, 95

R

retroviruses, 35
ribavirin, 106
risk factors, 59
Rizzetto, Mario, 25
RNA, 30, 35, 36
rubella, 35, 76
rubella virus, 36

S

safer sex, 88
salmonella, 103
sanitation, 43, 51
Schiff, Eugene R., 37
Seeff, Leonard B., 47, 48
serum hepatitis, 32, 45
sewage, 50
sex differences, 100
sexual activity, 51, 56, 58, 80
sexual transmission, 88
Shafritz, David A., 11, 84
shellfish, 51
snakes, 47
squirrels, 47
statisics, 10, 11, 13, 39, 40, 41, 42, 43,
    45, 47, 53, 55, 58, 67, 79, 82, 84,
    92, 93, 96
steroid hormones, 100
Stevens, Cladd, 55

symptoms, 7, 27–28, 37–41, 61

T

tattoo, 90
Taylor, John, 101
T cells, 42
thymus, 42
Tiber River, *44*
togaviruses, 35
toxic hepatitis, 28, 30
transaminases, 62
transgenic mice, 99, 100, 101
transmission, 7, 17, 50–60, 98
treatment, 7, 69–73
Tylenol, 30

V

vaccination, 79, *83*, 84, 92–98
vaccines, 7, 75–87, 106
vidarabine, 73
viral hepatitis, 30
viroids, 35

W

Werner, Barbara, 21
Werszberger, Alan, 85
Willowbrook State School, 14, 76
Wilson's disease, 36
woodchucks, 47, 99
World War I, 13
World War II, 13, *15*

Y

yeast cells, 82
yellow fever, 35, 76
yellow fever vaccine, 14
yellow fever virus, 36
yellow jaundice, 14